English
for
Science

English for Science

FRAN ZIMMERMAN

Illustrated by
Raquel Zimmerman

Prentice Hall Regents, Englewood Cliffs, New Jersey 07632

Library of Congress Cataloging-in-Publication Data

Zimmerman, Fran.
    English for science.

    1. Readers--Science. 2. English language--Technical
English. 3. English language--Textbooks for foreign
speakers. 4. Science--Terminology. I. Title.
PE1127.S3Z56 1989   428.2'4'0245   88-32376
ISBN 0-13-282179-6

Editorial/production supervision and interior design: Betsy Keefer
Cover design: Baldino Design
Manufacturing buyer: Laura Crossland

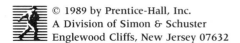 © 1989 by Prentice-Hall, Inc.
A Division of Simon & Schuster
Englewood Cliffs, New Jersey 07632

Printed in the United States of America
10 9 8 7 6 5 4 3 2 1

ISBN 0-13-282179-6

Prentice-Hall International (UK) Limited, *London*
Prentice-Hall of Australia Pty. Limited, *Sydney*
Prentice-Hall Canada, Inc., *Toronto*
Prentice-Hall Hispanoamericana, S.A., *Mexico*
Prentice-Hall of India Private Limited, *New Delhi*
Prentice-Hall of Japan, Inc., *Tokyo*
Simon & Schuster Asia Pte. Ltd., *Singapore*
Editora Prentice-Hall do Brasil, Ltda., *Rio de Janeiro*

For my father,
and in memory of my mother
    who taught me to think critically

Brief Contents

Contents

4 HYPOTHESIZING: *Motion and Gravity*   52

7 GIVING EVIDENCE: *Smoking, Drugs, and Alcohol*   96

10   REPORTING: *The Origin of Life*   141

Preface

English for Science is an English language text for use in secondary school, community college, or adult education programs to prepare students to participate in basic science courses. The text is designed for intermediate and advanced students of English as a second language. It integrates the four basic language skills—reading, writing, listening, and speaking—to facilitate the leap from basic English to academic English and to prepare students to comprehend and use college-level science material. The project evolved from a study of the needs of students at the American Language Institute in San Diego. Although the book focuses on science, most of the skills taught are appropriate preparation for any academic course of study. Similarly, although intended for non-native speakers, most of the material is adaptable for remedial classes for native speakers as well.

THEMATIC CONTENT

The unifying theme of *English for Science* is the scientific method, and the book aims to develop concepts of critical thinking and inquiry. The chapters are organized around the rhetorical functions used in scientific study (for example, classifying, comparing, and defining). Each rhetorical function is introduced in a short reading passage and developed further in a longer reading and a lecture. As far as possible, reading and writing skills are introduced as they relate to the rhetorical function.

Topics were selected from the general science curriculum to serve as vehicles for presenting the rhetorical functions, syntactic constructions, and vocabulary used frequently in scientific discourse. The non-native speaker may be familiar with the science concepts that are covered but not know how to express them in English. The focus of the book, however, is always on language rather than science, and there is no attempt to cover any scientific topic thoroughly. No previous science knowledge is needed by the teacher or student.

ORGANIZATION OF THE TEXT

There are twelve chapters in the book. Each chapter has six main sections: Introduction, Using English to . . . (classify, compare, and so on), Reading Skills, Listening Skills, Discussion Points, and Writing Skills.

Introduction

Each chapter begins by introducing the rhetorical function, relating it to the scientific method, and presenting it in a short reading.

Using English to . . .

This section begins with an explanation of the rhetorical function, using examples from the short reading. In most chapters the explanation is followed by a chart of sentence patterns that show how the function may be expressed. This chart is not meant to list all possible patterns, and in some chapters the chart is omitted because the topics do not lend themselves to any particular syntactic structure. The next item in the section is a group of practice exercises, sequenced to enable students to progress from identifying the function to using it. Grammatical structures that occur frequently in science texts are also included in this section when they serve a communicative purpose related to the rhetorical function.

Reading Skills

This section first presents strategies for students to use in expanding their vocabularies on an ongoing basis. Word roots and affixes introduced are those commonly occurring in scientific terminology (for example, *hydro-*, *dyna-*). Next, the section previews the vocabulary from the long reading. The object is to develop a basic vocabulary that would be assumed at the college-entry level. Accordingly, words selected for study are science-related terms that would be known to a native-speaking, first-year college student (for example, *flammable*, *dehydrate*, *transparent*, *combustion*, *dilute*, *inertia*). No specialized or rare words are used in any of the readings or lectures.

The rest of the section is devoted to a long reading passage and the development of useful reading skills, such as scanning, distinguishing fact from opinion, making inferences, and drawing conclusions.

Listening Skills

This section comprises a vocabulary preview, a note-taking hint, a practice exercise involving listening to a lecture and taking notes, and a comprehension exercise. Note-taking is frequently identified, by native and non-native speakers alike, as the most difficult part of academic study; yet it is a critical skill because many instructors do not base their lectures on textbooks.

Since ESL students at this reading level vary widely in their ability to comprehend lectures in English, some students may need to hear the lecture more than once. Following the comprehension exercise, all students should hear the lecture again without looking at their notes, to reinforce what they have learned and to ensure that comprehension is oral and not just visual.

Discussion Points

Most of the discussion points provide opportunity to apply the rhetorical function orally, in a relatively unstructured framework. In many chapters the topics serve as springboards for conversation practice, developing ideas that may be used in the writing lesson.

Writing Skills

Finally, students have the chance to extend the written use of the rhetorical function beyond the sentence level. The focus is on developing a paragraph with a main point and support material. In a few chapters students develop a longer passage and write a conclusion. The topics are frequently those already discussed in class. Although broad enough to encompass a variety of interests, the suggested topics are not intended to indicate all the possibilities. Students should be allowed to develop related topics of their own choice.

INSTRUCTOR'S MANUAL

The Instructor's Manual that accompanies the book contains scripts for the lectures and answers to the exercises.

ACKNOWLEDGMENTS

My thanks to Dr. Ann Johns of San Diego State University for the inspiration to write the book and to my daughter Raquel for her imaginative illustrations.

And a special thanks to Harry for his constant support and encouragement, and for always having more faith in me than I had in myself.

F. Z.

Introduction to the Scientific Method

Understanding scientific material requires an awareness of the basic method used by scientists. Western science began with the ancient Greeks, who believed that there was order in the universe and that events in nature could be predicted. Democritus originated the idea of the atom, Aristarchus suggested that the earth moved around the sun, and Anaximander proposed that human beings had developed from simpler forms of life.

It is interesting to wonder how much more advanced we might be if the progress of science had been steady since antiquity. By now, we might have communicated with other worlds or discovered a cure for cancer. Instead, science made very little progress during the Middle Ages. People were opposed to new ideas. Scientists were even thrown into prisons for trying to uncover the secrets of the universe. The great Italian genius Galileo was threatened with death when he refused to take back his statement that the sun rather than the earth was the center of our universe. Even as late as the 1800s, French biologist Louis Pasteur was laughed at when he suggested that diseases are caused by living things that are too small to be seen and can float through the air.

Modern science advanced only when people learned to open their minds to new ideas and to make judgments based on facts that could be tested with experiments. A procedure known as the scientific method was developed for gathering and testing information. Each chapter in this book is based on some aspect of this method and how it is expressed in English.

chapter **1**

Classifying

The Composition of Matter

INTRODUCTION

The early stages of scientific research involve making observations and gathering information. However, merely collecting facts is not enough. The scientist needs to arrange and classify the facts and to find relationships among them.

The word *classification* comes from the word *class*—meaning a group of things that all have one important element in common. Scientists group related information into an array. Chemists, for example, cannot study every element, but can make generalizations by arranging all the elements into groups with related properties. Thus, if iodine is identified as belonging to the same group as chlorine and bromine, its properties can be predicted. Similarly, since there are several million kinds of plants and animals on earth, it is clearly impossible to study each one. However, by classifying an animal as a member of a particular group, or species, a biologist can predict its characteristics. Classification is thus very basic to scientific thought and expression.

Short Reading

Read the following passage and find out how matter may be classified.

The Nature of Matter

Everything around us consists of matter: this book, your body, the air you breathe, and the water you drink. Matter is anything that has weight or mass and takes up space.

3

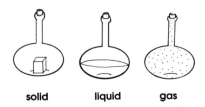

solid   liquid   gas

All matter may be classified as either solid, liquid, or gas. Solids are firm and have a definite form. Rubber, wood, glass, iron, cotton, and sand are all classified as solids. A considerable force would be needed to change the shape or volume of an iron bar, for example, because the atoms or molecules of a solid are densely packed and have very little freedom of movement.

Solids may be further divided into two classes: crystalline and amorphous. Rocks, wood, paper, and cotton are crystalline solids. Crystalline solids are made up of atoms arranged in a definite pattern. When these solids are heated, the change to a liquid, known as melting, is sharp and clear. Amorphous substances include rubber, glass, and sulfur. In these substances, the pattern of the atoms is not orderly, and when heated, they gradually soften.

Liquids, on the other hand, are not rigid. If water, milk, or oil is poured on a table, it will flow all over the surface. The atoms or molecules of liquids attract each other and thereby enable liquids to flow. But these atoms are loosely structured and do not keep their shape. Therefore a liquid will take the shape of any container in which it is poured. However, liquids have a definite volume; a quart of milk cannot fit in a pint container.

Gases, such as air, oxygen, and carbon dioxide, have no fixed shape or volume of their own. They diffuse or spread out to fill any container. If water is put into a tire, it will run to the bottom; if air is put into a tire, it fills the whole space inside the tire. The atoms or molecules of gases are widely spaced and move very rapidly. They either compress or expand to adapt to any area.

Everything we know is made of matter in solid, liquid or gaseous form. Later in this chapter, we will discuss other ways matter may be classified.

USING ENGLISH TO CLASSIFY

A classification includes:

1. a general class,
2. a specific item or items, and
3. a basis for classification, which is frequently *not* stated because it is understood or explained elsewhere.

Consider this sample sentence:

All matter may be classified as either solid, liquid, or gas.

The general class is *matter*. The specific items are *solid, liquid,* and *gas*. The basis for classification is the physical state of matter, which is not mentioned in the sentence.

But there is more than one way matter may be classified. For example, it may be classified on the basis of its chemical composition as either living or nonliving. For this reason, classification sentences frequently contain modals of possibility, such as *can, could,* or *may*.

CLASSIFYING FROM GENERAL TO SPECIFIC

All matter may be classified as either solid, liquid, or gas.
(Note that all matter is included in these three subdivisions.

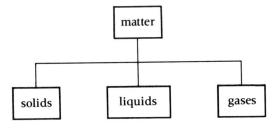

Solids may be further divided into two classes: crystalline and amorphous.

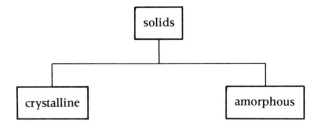

CLASSIFYING FROM SPECIFIC TO GENERAL

Rubber, wood, glass, iron, cotton, and sand are all classified as solids.
(When classifying from specific to general, the specific items do not necessarily cover all the subdivisions of the general category; that is, there are obviously other solids that are not included here.)

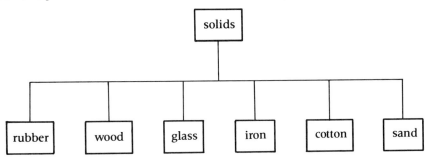

6 Classifying

Rocks, wood, paper, and cotton are crystalline solids.

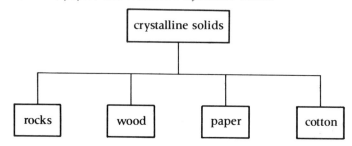

(Note that a classification is like an upside-down tree. The trunk of a tree is divided into large branches, each large branch is subdivided into smaller branches, and smaller branches may subdivide again into even smaller branches.)

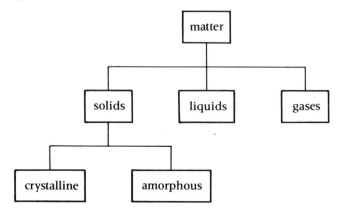

NOTES

1. The passive form is used frequently in sentences of classification and in all scientific writing because the emphasis in science is usually on the action, not on the person performing the action.
2. The present simple tense is the most commonly used tense in scientific writing because it expresses universals. (For example, *Water freezes at 0° C.*)
3. In a sentence like, *Oxygen is a gas,* only the meanings of the words *oxygen* and *gas* will reveal which is the general category and which is the specific item.

Sentence Patterns

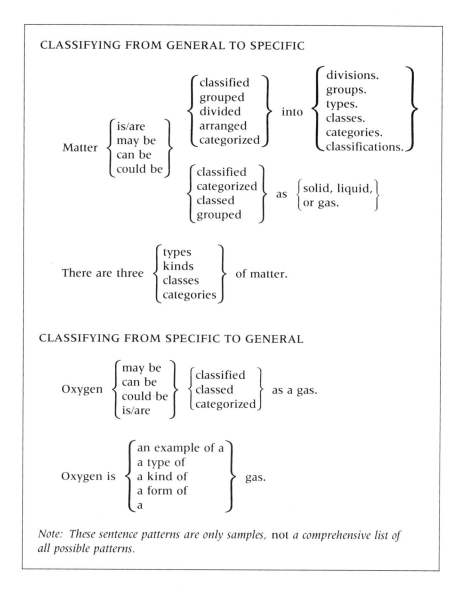

Note: *These sentence patterns are only samples,* **not** *a comprehensive list of all possible patterns.*

Identifying General and Specific Ideas.   In each sentence of classification, underline the general category once and each specific item twice. The first one is done as a sample.

1. Copper, lead, mercury, and silver are nonferrous substances.

2. Steel is an alloy.

3. Five important classes of compounds are acids, bases, salts, metallic oxides, and nonmetallic oxides.

4. A deer is a mammal.

5. Carbon exists in three forms: graphite, diamond, and amorphous.

6. Rocks are grouped into three categories: igneous, metamorphic, and sedimentary.

7. Coffee, tea, and paint are colloids.

8. Coal, wood, and oil may be classified as fuels.

9. Salts are inorganic compounds.

10. The two kinds of nucleic acids are deoxyribonucleic acid (DNA) and ribonucleic acid (RNA).

Transferring Information.   Read the following paragraph and find another way that matter may be classified. Then use the information in the passage to complete the chart.

ELECTRICAL CONDUCTIVITY

   Matter is frequently classified according to its electrical conductivity as a conductor, nonconductor, or semiconductor. Conductors have many electrons that are free to move and are useful in carrying, or conducting, electric current. All metals, particularly silver, copper, gold, and aluminum, are good conductors. Substances with few free electrons are called nonconductors, or insulators, because they do not carry electric charge and can be used to prevent electricity from flowing where it is not wanted. Air, wood, glass, and plastic are insulators. A few substances, like carbon, silicon, and germanium, do not fall into either of these categories. They are classed as semiconductors and are used in such electronic devices as transistor radios.

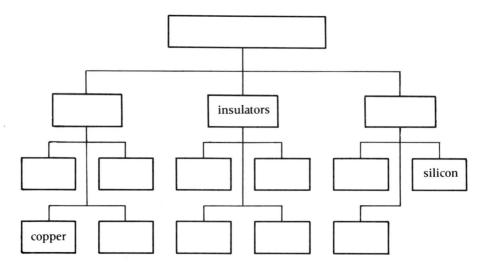

Completing Sentences. Complete the following sentences. Use the sentence patterns on p. 7 to help you. (Note that not all categories of plants and animals are listed here.)

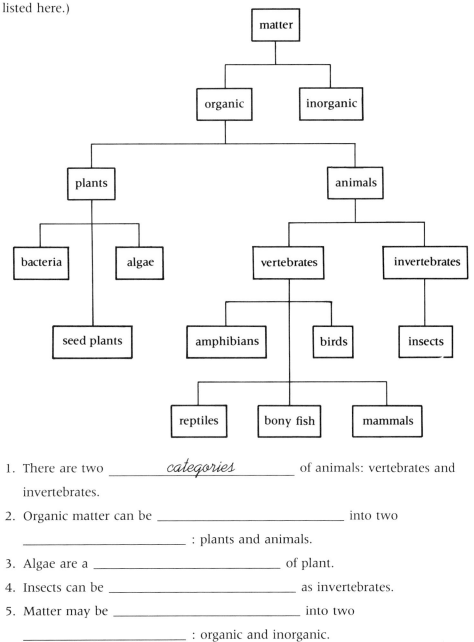

1. There are two _____ *categories* _____ of animals: vertebrates and invertebrates.

2. Organic matter can be _____ into two

   _____ : plants and animals.

3. Algae are a _____ of plant.

4. Insects can be _____ as invertebrates.

5. Matter may be _____ into two

   _____ : organic and inorganic.

6. Reptiles and amphibians are _____ as vertebrates.

7. Bacteria can be _____ as plants.

8. Invertebrates are a _____ of animal.

The Passive Voice

The passive form of a verb is used frequently in classifying and in all scientific writing. This is because the emphasis in science is usually on the action, *not* on the person performing the action. A sentence is *active* if the subject performs the action. It is *passive* if the subject receives the action. Look at these examples:

Scientists classify mercury as a metal. *(active)*

Mercury is classified as a metal. *(passive)*

The second sentence is preferred because it concentrates on how mercury is classified. (We know that scientists do the classifying.)

Formula for a passive sentence:

Object of verb from active sentence	+	proper form of verb *to be*	+	past participle of verb	+	by-phrase (optional)
Mercury		**is**		**classified**	**as a metal**	**(by scientists).**

If the action is in the present, use the present tense of the verb *to be*: *is* if the subject is singular, *are* if the subject is plural. If the action is in the past, use the past tense of the verb *to be*: *was* or *were*. When there is a modal, like *can* or *must*, use *can be* or *must be*. In the example above, the by-phrase (*by scientists*) is not used because it is understood. Here are some active sentences and their corresponding passive forms.

ACTIVE	PASSIVE
They grow coffee in Brazil and Columbia.	Coffee is grown in Brazil and Columbia.
We use lasers in place of needles in compact disc recordings.	Lasers are used in place of needles in compact disc recordings.
They discovered diamonds in South Africa in the nineteenth century.	Diamonds were discovered in South Africa in the nineteenth century.
James Watson and Francis Crick formulated the theory of the double helix.	The theory of the double helix was formulated by James Watson and Francis Crick.
Penicillin can cure pneumonia.	Pneumonia can be cured by penicillin.

Changing Active Voice to Passive Voice.   Change each of the following active sentences to the passive form. Be careful to choose the correct tense (present or past) and the correct number (singular or plural) for the verb *to be*. Include a by-phrase when you think the original subject (that is, the subject of the active sentence) is important to the passive sentence.

1. We extract sulfur from volcanic rock.
   Sulfur is extracted from volcanic rock.
2. Luigi Galvani invented the electric battery in 1786.
3. The authorities temporarily suspended the American space shuttle program after the accident in 1986.
4. Workers completed the Panama Canal in 1914.
5. The 1986 earthquake in Mexico City killed many people.
6. Chemists can extract nitrogen from the air by liquefication.
7. The white corpuscles in the blood destroy bacteria.
8. Meteors probably caused the craters on the moon.
9. Biologists sometimes classify simple, one-celled plants and animals together.
10. We may define artificial intelligence as the capacity of a computer to imitate human reasoning.

Using the Passive Voice.   Fill in the passive form of the verb in parentheses in the following sentences.

1. Each year, large amounts of carbon monoxide _____*are expelled*_____
   (expel) into the air by automobiles and factories.

2. The weights of the planets _____ (calculate) by
   Newton as a young man.

3. Water _____ (discover) under the Sahara Desert.

4. Coal _____ (produce) by plant matter of
   prehistoric times.

5. Soap _____ (manufacture) by boiling vegetable or
   animal fat with sodium or potassium hydroxide.

6. The hydrogen bomb _____ (call) a thermonuclear
   bomb because extremely high temperatures _____
   (need) to start the fusion process.

7. Human speech _____ (control) by a part of the
   brain called the cerebrum.

8. The concept of relativity _____ (propose) by Albert
   Einstein in 1905.

READING SKILLS

Vocabulary Building

A good vocabulary will help you with every aspect of communication; it will improve your reading and listening comprehension and will enable you to speak and write better. A good vocabulary will help you succeed in any profession.

When you first study a language, you learn everyday words that are repeated so often that they soon become part of your permanent vocabulary. However, after you have acquired a basic vocabulary, there is always a decline in vocabulary growth rate. Reading and speaking the language will increase your fluency but will *not* automatically increase your vocabulary. This is because the words you are learning appear less frequently and are thus more difficult to remember. At this stage of language development, you must make a special effort to acquire new words.

All the words in the vocabulary sections in this book were selected from the readings and lectures because they appear frequently in scientific discourse. There are no rare or specialized words. The word parts are also those found frequently in scientific terminology. In addition, the vocabulary sections contain strategies for continuing to build your vocabulary, that is, for making vocabulary growth a lifetime habit.

Vocabulary in Context.   Circle the letter of the answer that best matches the meaning of the italicized word as it is used in each of these sentences.

1. Atoms are *infinitesimal* in size.
   a. tiny   b. huge

2. Chemists study the composition of natural *substances.*
   a. materials   b. machines

3. The whale suddenly *emerged* from the water.
   a. arose   b. disappeared

4. All matter is either liquid, solid, or gas, and solids may be *subdivided* into crystalline and amorphous.
   a. built up   b. broken down

5. Plastic products are hard to dispose of because they are almost *indestructible.*
   a. unable to be destroyed   b. unable to be constructed

6. At one time the atom was thought to be *indivisible.*
   a. unable to be divided   b. unable to be seen

7. Einstein's ideas are too *abstract* for many people to understand.
   a. practical   b. theoretical

8. The *reaction* of iron and oxygen produces rust.
   a. chemical activity   b. separation

9. The airplane had to rely on radar in the *dense* fog.
   a. thick   b. thin

10. The moon *revolves* around the earth.
    a. stretches   b. circles

11. The mosquitoes showed their *attraction to* the light.
    a. dislike for   b. liking for

12. Some scientists suspect that the planet Uranus once *collided* with another object in space.
    a. crashed   b. orbited

Finding Main Ideas

Scientific writing consists mainly of concepts and material that supports those concepts. The concept is usually stated in a *topic sentence*, which acts as an umbrella to cover all the information in the paragraph. The rest of the paragraph contains supporting material—that is, information that explains, clarifies, or proves what is stated in the topic sentence.

The topic sentence is frequently but not always the first sentence of the paragraph. Sometimes it is the second sentence, appearing after an introduction or transition. At other times it is the last sentence, with other sentences leading up to it. Only rarely does it appear in the middle of the paragraph. All the sentences in the paragraph should relate to the topic sentence. (Occasionally a paragraph has no topic sentence because it contains support material for an earlier paragraph or acts as a transition between other paragraphs.)

In the following passage, put square brackets [] around the topic sentence of each paragraph.

Reading

The Infinitesimal Atom

There are over four million substances known to man. [Yet it is one of the amazing facts of science that all these substances are made up of only about 100 different varieties of matter, which are called elements.] Oxygen, hydrogen, gold, aluminum, sulfur, carbon, and chlorine are all examples of elements that combine in different ways to make the more than four million substances. Elements are made of particles called molecules, too tiny to be seen even with a powerful microscope. Molecules are made of even smaller particles called atoms. All the world is made of atoms.

The concept of atoms first emerged in ancient Greece. In 400 B.C. the philosopher Democritus theorized that matter could be divided into smaller and smaller particles until a point was reached beyond which no further subdivision was possible. These indestructible particles were called *atomos*, a Greek word meaning indivisible. We know today that atoms are so small that it would take more than a million of them to equal the thickness of this sheet of paper. Democritus' theory, however, was not universally accepted in the ancient world, for many believed in Aristotle's theory that matter is composed of four elements: earth, fire, air, and water.

During the Middle Ages in Europe, the concept of atoms was considered too abstract and was accordingly rejected. Finally, in 1804 the Englishman John Dalton formulated an atomic theory based on his experimentation. He claimed that all matter is made of atoms; that all atoms of a single element have the same shape, size, weight, and behavior; and that atoms of each element are different from those of any other element. He said that atoms are not created or destroyed but rather form new combinations in chemical reactions.

Dalton thought that atoms were solid, but today atoms are believed to consist mainly of space, with a dense nucleus at the center. The size of the nucleus inside an atom is comparable to the size of an ant on a football field. Each nucleus contains protons, which have a positive electric charge, and neutrons, which have no charge. The nucleus is surrounded by electrons, which have a negative electric charge. The number of protons equals the number of electrons in each atom, and therefore the entire atom has no charge. In 1913, the Danish physicist Niels Bohr proposed a model of the atom in which the electrons revolved around the nucleus like the planets revolve around the sun. Today the movement of electrons is thought to be more like bees hovering around a hive. The force of attraction between the positive protons in the nucleus and the negative electrons whirling around keeps the electrons in their paths.

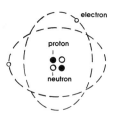

helium atom

What is it that makes iron hard, oxygen a gas, and mercury a liquid? The properties of an element are determined by the number of electrons in an atom, which is called the atomic number. All atoms of the same element are alike. If you've seen one atom of oxygen, you've seen them all. Hydrogen, the lightest element, has one electron and one proton. In fact, the hydrogen atom, the most common atom in the universe, is the basis on which our entire universe was formed. Oxygen has eight protons and eight electrons. Uranium, one of the heaviest elements, has 92 protons and 92 electrons.

All the world is made of atoms: Everything we see and know of is made of the billions and billions of these infinitesimal specks of matter. All life exists because atoms are continually moving, combining, separating, colliding, giving off energy, and absorbing energy.

Understanding the Reading.   Each of the following statements is inconsistent with the information in the previous passage. Test your reading comprehension by finding and correcting each error.

1. Molecules are even smaller than atoms.
   Atoms are even smaller than molecules.
2. The concept of the atom did not exist before 1804.
3. In ancient Greece, everyone believed Aristotle's theory that matter is composed of four elements: earth, fire, air, and water.
4. During the Middle Ages, the atomic theory was widely accepted.
5. John Dalton theorized that atoms are composed of electrons, protons, and neutrons.
6. The size of a nucleus inside an atom is equal to the size of an ant.
7. Atoms are densely packed with protons, neutrons, and electrons.
8. Neutrons have a negative electric charge.
9. Each atom is neutral because the number of its protons equals the number of its neutrons.
10. Niels Bohr proposed a model of the atom with the electrons revolving around the planets.
11. Electrons are kept in their paths by the force of gravity.
12. The atomic number of an element is the total of the number of electrons and the number of protons.
13. All the atoms of a single element are different.
14. Atoms of hydrogen are identical to atoms of oxygen.
15. The oxygen atom is the most common atom in the universe.

LISTENING SKILLS

Vocabulary in Context.   Circle the letter of the answer that best matches the meaning of the italicized word as it is used in each of these sentences.

1. Water *decomposes* into hydrogen and oxygen.
   a. separates   b. evaporates
2. Diamonds are expensive partly because they are so *rare*.
   a. scarce   b. abundant

3. The device was driven by *mechanical* energy.
   a. machine   b. electrical

4. Although hydrogen and oxygen have some similarities, each has
   characteristics that are *distinct*.
   a. similar   b. different

5. Sodium and chlorine are the *constituents* of salt.
   a. components   b. characteristics

6. Oxygen is a very *active* element that combines readily with other elements.
   a. stable   b. unstable

7. Some mushrooms are safe to eat, and others are *poisonous*.
   a. delicious   b. deadly

8. It was important to keep the temperature *constant* throughout the
   experiment.
   a. unchanging   b. changing

9. The outcome of an experiment is affected by *variables*.
   a. substances   b. changing factors

10. Besides nitrogen and oxygen, there is a small *proportion* of other gases in the
    air.
    a. quality   b. quantity

11. The noble gases are a group of gases with *homogeneous* properties.
    a. similar   b. different

12. A mosquito is *categorized* as an insect.
    a. classified   b. described

13. A flower can only *retain* its beauty for a short time.
    a. keep   b. lose

Note-Taking

Many people like to take a camera when they make a trip partly because they
know that they will remember the people and places they have recorded on film
and forget much of the rest. The notes you take during a lecture are like the
photographs you take on a trip. What you record, you will retain; most of the rest,
you will forget. Without notes, in a short while you will undoubtedly forget most
of the material presented in a lecture, even when the subject matter is interesting
to you. Just as with pictures, your goal is to record as many important points as
clearly and specifically as possible. Note-taking will *not* interfere with your listening.
On the contrary, it will help you to focus on what is being said and avoid letting
your mind wander. The succeeding chapters contain suggestions for good note-
taking.

Take notes as you listen to the lecture "The Chemistry of Matter," and then use
your notes to complete the next exercise.

Using Your Notes to Classify. Use the information from the lecture to classify each of these statements as describing an element (*E*), mixture (*M*), or compound (*C*).

___*M*___ 1. Its constituents may be present in any proportion.

_____ 2. Its constituents cannot be separated by mechanical means.

_____ 3. Alcohol is an example of one.

_____ 4. It cannot be broken down into simpler substances by ordinary chemical means.

_____ 5. There is more than one type of atom within each molecule.

_____ 6. It retains the properties of its constituents.

_____ 7. Milk is an example of one.

_____ 8. Carbon is an example of one.

_____ 9. The law of definite composition applies.

_____ 10. There are only about 92 found in nature.

_____ 11. Its characteristics are different from those of its constituents.

_____ 12. They are frequently categorized as metals and nonmetals.

DISCUSSION POINTS

1. How might you classify the students in this class or school?
2. What are some ways you could classify foods? fabrics? cars? schools? films? cities? academic subjects? animals? jobs? the people of a town or country? music?
3. A nutritionist might be interested in classifying foods according to calories, sodium content, cholesterol content, sugar content, vitamin content, and the like. This information would be needed to prescribe a diet for a specific person. What types of classification might interest a biologist? a chemist? a meteorologist? a psychologist? a police detective? a football player?

WRITING SKILLS

Topic Sentences

In English, written material is organized into paragraphs. Each paragraph expresses a complete thought. This central thought or idea is summarized in the topic sentence, which should cover everything that is in the paragraph and *only* what is in the paragraph.

The topic sentence may appear at the beginning of the paragraph to announce the main idea. Or it may appear at the end to summarize that idea. The topic sentence unifies the paragraph and makes it clear and understandable to the reader. The rest of the sentences in the paragraph should give details that support, explain, or prove the main point.

The sample paragraph below is incomplete. Read it and think of a good topic sentence to unify it. Also, find the one sentence that does *not* belong in the paragraph.

Astronomers classify planets according to their positions in relation to the earth. Those that are inside the earth's orbit (that is, Mercury and Venus) are classed as inferior planets. All the others are called superior planets. Recent space explorations have uncovered no evidence of life on any of these planets. Planets may also be classified according to their size and mass. Mercury, Venus, Mars, and Pluto are sometimes called the terrestrial planets because they are similar in size to the earth. Jupiter, Saturn, Uranus, and Neptune are the major or larger planets. Jupiter is the largest, followed by Saturn and then the "twins," Uranus and Neptune.

Which of the following is the best topic sentence for this paragraph?

1. Planets may be classified according to size and mass.
2. Planets may be classified according to position or size.
3. Scientists classify many things in the universe.
4. Planets may be classified according to position.

Sentences 1 and 4 are too narrow to be the topic sentence, for neither covers all the information in the paragraph. Sentence 3 is not the best because it is too broad; it is not specific to this paragraph. Sentence 2 is the best topic sentence because it announces exactly what the paragraph is about—no more, no less.

Which sentence does not belong in the paragraph? The sentence that begins *Recent space explorations . . .* is *not* relevant to the topic of classification and therefore should not be included.

Writing a Paragraph of Classification

Write a paragraph of classification based on one of the Discussion Points that interests you. Start the paragraph with a topic sentence that

1. states the main idea,
2. is broad enough to cover everything in the paragraph, and
3. is specific enough to cover only what is in the paragraph.

The rest of the sentences should provide the details that relate to, support, or explain the topic sentence.

Always reread your paragraph, preferably after some time has passed. Check to see that every sentence is related to the topic sentence.

chapter 2

Comparing
The Elements

INTRODUCTION

Scientists try to organize information by seeking relationships. Classification is one way of arranging information. Comparing is another.

Comparisons not only arrange information but also expand it. When prehistoric human beings noticed that wood burns and stone does not, they were making an important step toward advancing scientific knowledge. Often comparisons enable us to solve problems. For example, to determine which substance to use for electrical wiring, various metals are compared for electrical conductivity, cost, availability, and the like.

Comparisons provide a new perspective on information. For example, the fact that an ant can carry a crumb of bread only becomes impressive when the crumb is discovered to be three times the weight of the ant. The fact that water expands when it becomes solid is more interesting when comparisons show that all other liquids contract, or take up less space, as they solidify. It was a comparison of the habits of lung cancer victims with those of the general population that led to the discovery of a link between smoking and lung cancer. Comparisons are thus a part of every aspect of science.

Short Reading

Read the following passage and find as many comparisons as you can.

The Wonder Metals

The study of metals began in the Middle Ages when alchemists searched for a technique to convert ''base metals,'' like lead, to gold. They never succeeded in making gold but at least by experimenting with the metals (in contrast to the ancient Greeks, who only speculated about them) they made many discoveries.

All but 20 of the over 100 elements identified to date are metals but only 7 of these are common in the earth's crust. Iron, the most widely used metal, is rarely found in the free state (not combined with other metals) and must be extracted from naturally occurring compounds (ores) such as hematite, magnetite, and pyrite. The beautiful colors of rocks are due almost entirely to these iron compounds. In fact, iron pyrite is often called fool's gold because of the similarity of its color to gold. Iron is very strongly magnetic, and the fact that the earth is a magnet itself tipped scientists off to the fact that iron is a major component of the earth's core, or center.

Pure iron is a relatively soft, silvery metal that is very active chemically (that is, it combines with oxygen to corrode or form rust). It is usually mixed with other elements or compounds to form alloys such as steel, stainless steel, or cast iron, which are more durable and rust resistant than pure iron.

Aluminum is the most abundant metal, but it was not used until a century ago because it is so active chemically and difficult to extract. Like iron it is soft, but in contrast to iron and steel, aluminum is very light and more resistant to corrosion. These qualities make it useful for airplanes, trains, automobiles, rockets, and house siding.

In the 1940s, magnesium emerged as an important metal. Although it is less abundant in the earth, more chemically active, and harder to extract than aluminum, it is present in sea water and that means there is almost an endless supply of it.

In the space age, the extraordinary properties of titanium have made it the new wonder metal. Lighter and stronger than steel, it is more resistant to corrosion and able to withstand heat.

The remaining major metals are sodium, potassium, and calcium, all too active chemically (they react violently with water) for use in construction.

USING ENGLISH TO COMPARE

Comparing is examining two or more items to discover their similarities and differences. Comparing may but does not always concentrate on similarities. Contrasting concentrates on differences.

COMPARING SIMILARITIES

. . .iron pyrite is often called fool's gold because of the similarity of its color to gold.

color: iron pyrite ≈ gold

Like iron it [aluminum] is soft. . . .

softness: iron ≈ aluminum

CONTRASTING DIFFERENCES

Iron, the most widely used metal. . . .

use: iron > all other metals

Pure iron is a relatively soft, silvery metal. . . .

softness: iron > many other metals

Aluminum is the most abundant metal. . . .

abundance: aluminum > all other metals

. . .in contrast to iron and steel, aluminum is very light and more resistant to corrosion. . . .

lightness: aluminum > iron and steel

resistance to corrosion: aluminum > iron and steel

Although it [magnesium] is less abundant in the earth . . . than aluminum. . . .

abundance: magnesium < aluminum

Sentence Patterns

COMPARING SIMILARITIES

Magnesium is $\begin{cases} \text{like} \\ \text{similar to} \\ \text{comparable to} \\ \text{as important as} \end{cases}$ aluminum.

Magnesium $\begin{cases} \text{resembles} \\ \text{parallels} \end{cases}$ aluminum in many ways.

CONTRASTING DIFFERENCES

Iron $\begin{cases} \text{is unlike} \\ \text{is different from} \\ \text{differs from} \end{cases}$ aluminum.

$\left.\begin{array}{l} \text{Unlike iron,} \\ \text{In contrast to iron,} \\ \text{Compared to iron,} \\ \text{In comparison to iron,} \end{array}\right\}$ aluminum is light.

Iron is $\begin{cases} \text{heavier than} \\ \text{less abundant than} \\ \text{not as soft as} \end{cases}$ aluminum.

Iron is a $\begin{cases} \text{relatively} \\ \text{comparatively} \end{cases}$ soft metal.

Understanding Comparisons.   Read the passage below to determine the order of the seven italicized metals according to their melting points. List the metal with the *highest* melting point *first*.

The melting point of *platinum* is high compared to most metals but not as high as that of *chromium*. The melting point of *zinc* is less than half the melting point of *gold* and approximately three times the melting point of *sodium*. *Mercury* has the lowest melting point of all the metals. *Copper* and gold have similar melting points, but the melting point of copper is slightly higher than gold and lower than platinum.

Using a Table. Tables, charts, and graphs organize information to enable us to see comparisons readily. Circle the answer that best completes the statement according to the information in the chart.

The Physical Properties of Six Metals

Metal	Specific Gravity	Melting Point (°C)	Boiling Point (°C)	Atomic Radius (Å)	Ionic Radius (Å)
Group I					
Copper	8.9	1083	2595	1.17	.96
Silver	10.5	960	2212	1.34	1.26
Gold	19.3	1063	2966	1.34	1.37
Group II					
Zinc	7.14	420	907	1.25	.74
Cadmium	8.65	321	765	1.41	.96
Mercury	13.60	− 38.87	357	1.44	1.1

1. The atomic radius of cadmium is _____ that of mercury.
   a. as high as   (b.) not as high as

2. _____ mercury, cadmium has a high boiling point.
   a. Like   b. Compared to

3. The specific gravity of cadmium and copper are _____ .
   a. similar   b. identical

4. Compared to the other metals on this table, gold has _____ specific gravity.
   a. a relatively high   b. the highest

5. The properties of cadmium and zinc are _____ .
   a. comparable   b. identical

6. Copper and gold have _____ high boiling points.
   a. comparatively   b. equally

7. The melting points of the Group II metals are _____ those of Group I.
   a. lower than   b. as low as

8. The ionic radius of copper is _____ to that of cadmium.
   a. similar   b. equal

Creating Sentences.   Write a sentence comparing the items in each of these pairs. There is more than one way to write each answer.

1. surface temperature: Mercury—350°C
                           Venus—475°C

The surface temperature of Mercury is lower than that of Venus.

2. maximum life span: kangaroo—16 years
                         cat—23 years
3. calories: apple (medium)—75
               egg—70
4. diameter: moon—3,480 km
               earth—12,800 km
5. gestation period: elephant—21 months
                       giraffe—14–15 months
6. percent of world's water: Pacific Ocean—46%
                               Atlantic Ocean—22.9%

Creating Comparisons.   Compare the items in each of these pairs orally in one or two sentences. Note that the items have something in common, for otherwise there would be no point in comparing them. A good way to make a comparison is to begin with what they have in common. Include at least one way the items are similar and one way they are different. For example, to compare tea and coffee, you might say, "Both coffee and tea are drinks, but coffee is made from a bean and tea is prepared from leaves."

1. a telescope and a microscope
2. a submarine and a dolphin
3. a computer and a calculator
4. a desert and a jungle
5. a photocopier and an x-ray machine

Like *and* As

Comparisons frequently use the words *like* and *as. Like* is used before a noun or pronoun:

He thinks like a scientist.

But if the noun or pronoun is followed immediately by a verb, the word *as* is used:

Don't do as I do, do as I say.

As is also used before and after an adjective, like two slices of bread sandwiching in the adjective:

The night was *as* long *as* the day.
(The night and day were equally long.)

Silver is not *as* malleable *as* gold.
(Silver is less malleable than gold.)

Using **Like** *and* **As**.   Fill in the blanks in each of the following sentences with *as* or *like.*

1. Sodium, _____*like*_____ potassium, is an alkali metal.

2. The ancient Greek scientists did not experiment _____ modern scientists do.

3. Modern computers are not _____ large _____ the first computers.

4. _____ Galileo before him, Newton studied motion.

5. Cobalt is a heavy metal _____ nickel.

6. Helium is almost _____ light _____ hydrogen.

7. Nickel does not rust _____ iron does.

READING SKILLS

Vocabulary Building

Interrupting a reading or lecture to look up words in a dictionary will break your concentration. Therefore, when you read or hear a new word, you should always try to figure out its meaning from its context. Sometimes the sentence itself contains a definition:

Silver sulfide, a black chemical substance, forms on its surface.

At other times, the surrounding sentences or paragraph gives some indication of the meaning:

Gold is a ductile metal. One gram of gold can be drawn into a wire 1.8 miles in length.

From these two sentences, you can conclude that a ductile metal is one that can be stretched or pulled into wire.

In the vocabulary sections of each unit, you will have the chance to figure out word meanings from sentences. Then, in the readings and lectures, you can use other clues to help you understand the word.

Vocabulary in Context. Circle the letter of the answer that best matches the meaning of the italicized word as it is used in each of the following sentences.

1. Silicon is a nonmetallic element that is inexpensive because it is so *abundant* in minerals and rocks.
   a. rare   (b.) plentiful

2. When exposed to air and moisture, iron will *corrode*.
   a. rust   b. shine

3. When the flames subsided, the police investigated the cause of the *combustion*.
   a. burning   b. excitement

4. The *spontaneous* explosion caused a lot of damage.
   a. unplanned   b. planned

5. The room got stuffy and warm due to improper *ventilation*.
   a. heating   b. air circulation

6. Many lives could be saved if natural *phenomena* such as earthquakes and hurricanes could be predicted.
   a. resources   b. occurrences

7. There is oxygen in the *protoplasm* of all plants and animals.
   a. blood   b. living matter

8. Amphibians are *organisms* that live on land and in water.
   a. minerals   b. living things

9. Human *respiration* involves inhaling oxygen and exhaling carbon dioxide.
   a. breathing   b. circulation

10. *Inhaling* smoke is bad for your lungs.
    a. breathing out   b. breathing in

11. Larger vehicles *consume* more gasoline than smaller ones.
    a. use   b. save

12. Water is *vital* to all living things.
    a. necessary   b. useless

13. Heat can *convert* a solid to a liquid.
    a. condense   b. change

14. Farmers *fertilize* their soil to make it more productive.
    a. enrich   b. ruin

15. The ammonia was *diluted* in water to make it weaker.
    a. thinned   b. thickened

16. A *catalyst* speeds up a chemical reaction.
    a. chemical agent   b. forest animal

17. *Antibiotics* will cure many diseases but not the common cold.
    a. bacteria-killing drugs   b. pain-killing drugs

18. Today, local *anesthetics* are being used in place of general anesthetics for many operations.
    a. painkillers   b. stimulants

19. To obtain aluminum, metallurgists must *extract* it from bauxite.
    a. remove   b. destroy

20. Gasoline should be stored carefully because it is *flammable*.
    a. fireproof   b. able to catch fire easily

Skimming

When studying science, you will usually want to know if a reading passage contains the information that you need. In that case, it is advisable to skim the material *without* reading it all to get a general idea of its contents. To skim a passage:

1. Read the title and any subtitles, which are like little summaries.
2. Read the introduction.

3. Read the first sentence of every paragraph, which frequently, although not always, contains the main idea.
4. Read the summary or conclusion at the end of the passage.

Note: To skim a whole book, read the first paragraph and conclusion of each chapter.

Skim the following passage to discover its main topic and the information it contains. Then answer the following questions. Try to do this all in three and a half minutes. (You will be given time to read the passage thoroughly later.)

1. The main topic of this reading is:
   a. the industrial uses of oxygen, nitrogen, and hydrogen.
   b. how oxygen, nitrogen, and hydrogen differ from the other elements.
   c. the importance of oxygen, nitrogen, and hydrogen to living things.
   d. the differences between the three gases.
2. All of the following topics are discussed in the passage *except*:
   a. oxidation.
   b. a comparison of nitrogen and oxygen.
   c. the characteristics of hydrogen.
   d. the scientists who discovered each gas and the year of discoveries.

Reading

The Life-Supporting Gases

How long can a human being live without oxygen? What if there were no nitrogen in the air? Just how important is hydrogen?

Three of our most abundant and important elements are the gases oxygen, nitrogen, and hydrogen. Although they share many properties—all three are colorless, odorless, and tasteless at room temperature—each one is necessary to life in a unique way.

The same substance causes metals to corrode, wood to rot, apples to turn brown, paint to harden, gasoline to burn, and iron to rust. Fire cannot burn without it, and human beings cannot live without it. This substance is oxygen, an essential ingredient in air and water and the most abundant element in the earth's crust.

Oxygen is very active chemically, meaning that it readily combines with other substances in a process called oxidation. For example, iron combines with oxygen from the air to produce iron oxide, or rust. Food and water combine with oxygen to form decay. Vegetable oils used in paints combine with oxygen to harden. These are all examples of slow oxidation.

The rapid oxidation of fuels causes combustion, or fire. Sometimes a fire starts spontaneously. If a substance with a low kindling temperature, such as oily rags, newspapers, or grain, is heated in the absence of proper ventilation, oxidation may

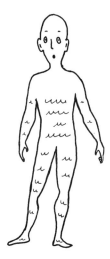

Our bodies are two-thirds water.

occur so rapidly that the substance bursts into flames. This phenomenon is called spontaneous combustion.

Oxygen is found in the protoplasm of all living organisms and is essential to respiration. Human beings cannot live more than five minutes without oxygen. We inhale oxygen, which passes into the bloodstream and is carried to the body tissues. There it combines with the food we consume, producing the energy we need to maintain our body temperature and to supply us with the strength for physical activity.

Nitrogen is also vital to living things. All plants and animals contain nitrogen compounds in which the nitrogen has been converted to its free state by a process called nitrogen fixation. Fertilizers contain nitrogen compounds to feed plants and help them to grow.

In contrast to oxygen, nitrogen is comparatively inactive; that is, it does not readily combine with other substances. Therefore, nitrogen does not support combustion. If there were no nitrogen to dilute the oxygen in the air we breathe, the combustion of fuel would be extremely fast, metals would corrode rapidly, and smoking would be impossible. When, however, with the help of high temperatures, electricity, and catalysts, nitrogen does react with other elements, it tends to be very powerful. Because many nitrogen compounds are unstable, they are used in explosives like TNT and gunpowder. Other compounds include drugs such as poisons, antibiotics, laughing gas (nitrous oxide), and anesthetics. Nitrogen can be extracted from the air by liquefying air.

Hydrogen is the most abundant element in the universe. The sun and stars are almost pure hydrogen. Our sun's source of energy is the conversion of hydrogen into helium. Hydrogen is also found in almost all plant and animal tissues. There are more atoms of hydrogen in our bodies than any other element because our bodies are about two-thirds water! Hydrogen is also found in most fuels and in all acids. It is the lightest known element and is highly flammable. Helium is almost as light as hydrogen but it is nonflammable.

Hydrogen and oxygen are the main constituents of the water we drink. Nitrogen and oxygen are the chief elements of the air we breathe. Our existence could not be possible without the presence of all three.

Understanding the Reading.   Each of the following statements is inconsistent with the information in the previous passage. After a careful reading of the passage, test your comprehension by finding the error in each statement and restating it correctly.

1. Oxygen, nitrogen, and hydrogen have similar properties, but only oxygen is essential to life.

   Oxygen, nitrogen, and hydrogen have similar properties, and all three are essential to life.

2. The substance that causes wood to rot is not the same as the one that causes apples to turn brown.
3. The decaying of food is an example of rapid oxidation.
4. It is impossible for a fire to start spontaneously.
5. Human beings can live up to 15 minutes without oxygen.
6. Nitrogen converts to a free state by a process called spontaneous combustion.
7. Compared to oxygen, nitrogen is very active.
8. If the air were pure oxygen, we could all smoke without harming our health.
9. Nitrogen is used in explosives because it is so stable.
10. Oxygen is the most abundant element in the universe.
11. Scientists do not know what the sun is made of.
12. Hydrogen is the most abundant element in our bodies because our bodies are mostly air.
13. In contrast to helium, hydrogen is nonflammable.
14. The essential ingredient in fertilizers is hydrogen.

LISTENING SKILLS

Vocabulary in Context.   Circle the letter of the answer that best matches the meaning of the italicized word as it is used in each of these sentences.

1. We polished the car to give the finish a *luster*.
   (a.) shine   b. dullness

2. The *scarcity* of oil caused the price to rise.
   a. shortage   b. abundance

3. Iron can be molded into different types of tools because it is so *malleable*.
   a. easily shaped   b. shiny

4. Copper is used for electric wiring because it is a good conductor and very *ductile*.
   a. breakable   b. stretchable

5. Stainless steel is a metal that *resists* rust.
   a. absorbs   b. withstands

6. The acid had caused *corrosion* in parts of the engine.
   a. rust   b. shine

7. Many synthetic fabrics are more *durable* than cotton and will not shrink or fade.
   a. beautiful   b. long lasting

8. Carbon is *alloyed* with iron to produce steel.
   a. replaced   b. combined

9. Silver needs to be polished frequently because it *tarnishes*.
   a. shines   b. blackens

10. Icebergs float on the *surface* of the ocean.
    a. bottom   b. top

11. The image of the house was *reflected* in the water.
    a. repeated   b. absorbed

12. The *properties* of all heavy metals are similar.
    a. uses   b. characteristics

13. Metals are *conductors* of heat and electricity.
    a. preventors   b. carriers

Note-Taking

The purpose of taking notes is to record the main ideas of a lecture in order to study or review them later. You will take better notes if you read your textbook chapter before your class lecture. Prereading is useful for all students but essential for those who are studying in a foreign language. First, prereading will introduce you to new terms so that when you hear them in class you will recognize them and be able to understand and record them. Second, prereading will familiarize you with the basic concepts of the lesson. This will help you follow the development of the topic and focus on what you need to write down for recall.

Take notes as you listen to the lecture "The Precious Metals," and then use your notes to complete the next exercise.

Understanding the Lecture. Use your notes to determine whether each of the following statements is true (*T*) or false (*F*) according to the information in the lecture.

____T____ 1. Gold, silver, and copper are valued for their luster and scarcity.

_____ 2. Newton was the first to succeed in changing base metals into gold.

_____ 3. Copper is as malleable and ductile as gold.

_____ 4. Gold is the most chemically active of all the metals.

_____ 5. Gold has a beautiful luster but it is not as durable as silver.

_____ 6. In contrast to gold, silver tarnishes.

_____ 7. Pure silver is a relatively soft metal.

_____ 8. Silver is used for photographic film because some silver compounds reflect light.

_____ 9. The properties of silver resemble those of gold and copper.

_____ 10. Gold is not used for electric wiring because it is not ductile.

_____ 11. Copper is used for electric wiring because it is a better conductor than silver.

_____ 12. Bronze, an alloy of tin and copper, is harder than either tin or copper.

_____ 13. Gold, silver, and copper are among our most abundant metals.

DISCUSSION POINTS

To compare items, begin with their similarities and then point out their differences. Avoid vague statements such as, "Car A is better than Car B." In what specific ways are they different? Does Car A have a more powerful motor? a stronger body? a faster pickup? *Be specific.*

1. Compare a computer and the human brain. Computers have been programmed to translate from one language to another, to play chess, and to solve complex mathematical problems. Will they ever be able to think? Will they be able to analyze, evaluate, make decisions, and make judgments? Will they be able to design, imagine, or create?
2. Compare a sport or game that is popular in this country with one that is popular in your country.
3. Compare the foods of two countries you know. Why are they different?
4. Compare an American car with one from another country. Consider their power, reliability, comfort, cost, appearance, and workmanship.

5. Compare a painting and a photograph. What can each do that the other cannot?

WRITING SKILLS

Comparing

Scientific writing often requires a discussion of the similarities and differences among two or more items. There are two basic methods of comparing items:

Method 1: Describe the characteristics of the first item and then the characteristics of the second.

Method 2: Compare both items one characteristic at a time.

Read the examples below and determine which method is used in each.

The difference between analog and digital data is not always clearly understood, but it can be demonstrated. As an example, think of an elevator. There are two ways you can think about its position. If you ask how high up it is from the basement, and measure with a ruler, you will be measuring its analog position. That is, the length the ruler measures—47 feet, $6\frac{7}{8}$ inches (approximately 14.5 m)—is an analog of how high up the elevator really is. If you tell what floor it's on, you are giving its digital position. It is either on the third floor or the fourth. It may be halfway in between, but there is no floor numbered $3\frac{1}{2}$. Its height varies continuously and can never be measured precisely, while its floor number is discrete, one or another, even if you have to "watch your step."

Allen Wold, *Computer Science*
(New York: Franklin Watts, 1984),
pp. 28–29

Deuterium and tritium are two rare forms of hydrogen. Tritium fuses more easily than deuterium, although both fuse more easily than ordinary hydrogen. Deuterium is rare, but it is stable. Tritium, on the other hand, is radioactive and can only be found in traces on the earth. However, it can be manufactured by bombarding lithium with neutrons, although this method makes it more expensive than deuterium.

The first paragraph uses Method 1. Analog data is described first and digital data second.

The second paragraph uses Method 2. The two items are compared characteristic by characteristic: first for fusibility, then for stability, and finally for cost. Frequently, a combination of Methods 1 and 2 are used.

Transition Words

In all writing, it is very important to show how the ideas are related. Words that clarify these relationships are called transition words. Transition words that are used to show contrast include *although, but, however, in contrast, on the other hand, even though, nevertheless, on the contrary, yet, in spite of* and *despite*. Other transition words such as *similarly, likewise, in the same way, moreover, also, furthermore*, and *besides* express the comparison of like items.

Writing a Paragraph of Comparison

Write a paragraph of comparison on one of the Discussion Points. Begin with a topic sentence that states the main idea. Then develop the rest of the paragraph to support the main idea, using Method 1 or Method 2 described above.

chapter 3

Cause and Effect
Color, Light, and Sound

INTRODUCTION

The process of seeking relationships among scientific facts includes looking for cause and effect. The fifth-century B.C. Greek philosopher Leucippus suggested that there is causality in nature, that is, that every natural event has a natural cause. All science is based on this assumption. For example, something causes apples to fall, planets to stay in their orbits, the sun to emit energy, and a baby to be born with a defect.

Scientists must be careful, however, not to assume that one event caused another just because they happened in sequence. If there is an earthquake the day a comet passes near the earth, it cannot be assumed that the two events are related.

Sometimes the effect of one occurrence becomes the cause of a second event, and the effect of the second becomes the cause of a third. A nuclear reaction is an example of this kind of causal link. As one uranium atom is split, it releases neutrons that in turn split other uranium atoms. The result is a continuous chain reaction of causes and effects. It is the job of science to connect situations and events and thereby discover the how's and why's of our world.

Short Reading

Read the passage below to discover what causes us to see different colors.

The Nature of Color

Why is the sky blue and the grass green? Why isn't the sky green and the grass blue? And why is a rose red instead of purple? What we see as color is the way our brains respond to the different wavelengths of light.

Light is a form of electromagnetic energy that travels very quickly on different frequencies, or wavelengths, which we see as different colors. For example, a wavelength of 400 nanometers (nm) causes us to see violet. A wavelength of 660 nm causes us to see red. The color brown is induced by the mixing of wavelengths. Yellow can be produced by either its own wavelength or a mixture of the wavelengths for red and green. Our sky looks blue because molecules of oxygen and nitrogen in the air scatter more blue wavelengths than any other color.

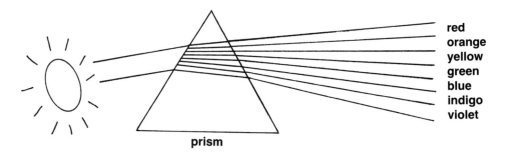

White light results from a mixing of the wavelengths of all colors. Sir Isaac Newton discovered that when sunlight passed through a glass prism, the white light dispersed into a spectrum of colored light. Newton then allowed the spectrum to pass through a second prism and the colors recombined, producing a beam of white light. This simple experiment demonstrated that white light contains all the colors of the spectrum. A beautiful and dramatic example of this occurs when sunlight falls on drops of water in the air after a rain. The beam of white sunlight spatters into a rainbow of colors.

Certain colors are invisible to human eyes. Wavelengths shorter than that of violet produce ultraviolet light that can damage skin cells. Wavelengths longer than that of the color red produce infrared light, radio waves, x-rays, and gamma rays. We cannot see colors produced by these wavelengths, but we can measure and use their energy.

USING ENGLISH TO SHOW CAUSE AND EFFECT

Causes and effects connect events or situations. Causes explain why something happens. Effects describe outcomes.

. . . a wavelength of 400 nanometers (nm) causes us to see violet.

CAUSE   EFFECT

wavelength of 400 nm $\longrightarrow$ **we see violet**

The color brown is induced by the mixing of wavelengths.
(Sometimes the effect precedes the cause in the sentence. By definition, however, causes always precede effects.)

EFFECT   CAUSE

the color brown $\longleftarrow$ **a mixing of wavelengths**

Yellow can be produced by either its own wavelength or a mixture of the wavelengths for red and green.
(Causes and effects are often complex. One effect may be produced by many causes, and one cause may produce many effects.)

EFFECT   CAUSES

yellow $\longleftarrow$ **its own wavelength**

OR

**a mixture of the wavelengths
for red and green**

Wavelengths shorter than that of violet produce ultraviolet light that can damage skin cells.
(An effect can become a cause. Sometimes there is a cycle of causes and effects.)

CAUSE   EFFECT/CAUSE   EFFECT

wavelengths $\longrightarrow$ **ultraviolet light** $\longrightarrow$ **damaged skin**
shorter than that   **cells**
of violet

White light results from a mixing of the wavelengths of all colors. . . . The beam of white sunlight splatters into a rainbow of colors.
(Sometimes there is a correlation between two events, that is, one event always accompanies the other, whether or not there is a causal connection.

CAUSE/EFFECT   CAUSE/EFFECT

**white light $\longrightarrow$ a mixture of the
                 wavelengths of all colors**

Sentence Patterns

A mixing of all wavelengths $\left\{ \begin{array}{l} \text{causes} \\ \text{results in} \\ \text{produces} \\ \text{induces} \end{array} \right\}$ a white light.

White light is $\left\{ \begin{array}{l} \text{caused by} \\ \text{due to} \\ \text{induced by} \\ \text{a result of} \\ \text{produced by} \end{array} \right\}$ a mixing of wavelengths.

$\left. \begin{array}{l} \text{If} \\ \text{When} \\ \text{As} \end{array} \right\}$ all the wavelengths are mixed, a white light is produced.

A white light is produced $\left\{ \begin{array}{l} \text{if} \\ \text{when} \\ \text{as} \end{array} \right\}$ all the wavelengths are mixed.

Note: Some of the above are also predictions and can be expressed with the future tense. For example, "If all the wavelengths are mixed, a white light will be produced." (Predictions will be discussed further in Chapter 12.)

Identifying Cause and Effect.   The Roman orator Cicero wrote, "The causes of events are ever more interesting than the events themselves." In each of the following sentences, underline the cause once and the effect twice.

1. When copper is heated to 1083° C, it melts.

2. Changes occur in plants when they absorb energy from the sun.

3. The rotation of a compass needle is due to the earth's magnetic field.

4. Ashes result from the burning of wood.

5. Acids turn litmus paper red.

6. Rubbing a comb with a cloth produces a negative electric charge.

7. Fast-moving charged particles induce the ionization of atoms.

8. The ocean's tides are caused by the gravitational pull of the moon.

9. The more iron is exposed to moist air, the more it rusts.

10. Color is produced by the reflection of light.

Understanding Paraphrases.   Circle the letter of the answer that best matches the meaning of each of these sentences.

1. Increasing the temperature increases the rate of a chemical reaction.
    a. Chemical reactions cause an increase in temperature.
    b. An increase in the rate of a chemical reaction may be caused by increasing the temperature.

2. Ions are formed when an acid is dissolved in water.
    a. Ions cause an acid to be dissolved in water.
    b. Dissolving an acid in water causes ions to be formed.

3. The closer the lines of force, the stronger the electric field.
    a. When the lines of force are closer, the electric field is stronger.
    b. The lines of force cause the electric field to be stronger.

4. Heating solid carbon dioxide (dry ice) produces a gas.
    a. A gas results from heating solid carbon dioxide.
    b. Carbon dioxide turns solid when heated.

5. Mirages are caused by light rays bending in the air.
    a. Mirages can result from light rays bending in the air.
    b. Mirages cause light rays to bend in the air.

6. Vibrations in the air cause the sound of the wind.
    a. Air vibrations are a result of the wind.
    b. The sound of the wind is a result of air vibrations.

Subordination

Subordination, or the connection of two clauses so that one is subordinate to or less important than the other, is frequently used in sentences that show cause and effect. Subordination allows you to focus on the important part of the sentence by putting it in a *main clause*, while the less important idea appears in the subordinate or secondary clause:

Human beings cannot live on the moon because there is no air or water there.

The main clause of this sentence, *human beings cannot live on the moon*, is *independent*, which means that it can stand alone as a sentence. The secondary, or less important, idea (*because there is no air or water on the moon*) is expressed in the *subordinate clause*, which is *dependent* on the main clause. It cannot stand alone as a sentence because it does not express a complete thought by itself.

Notice that the word *because* acts as a connector between the meanings of the two clauses. The connecting word always introduces the subordinate or less important clause. Note also that the clauses may be reversed. It is equally correct to say, *Because there is no air or water there, human beings cannot live on the moon.* Now the subordinate clause appears before the main clause. And, although the word *because* is not located between the clauses, it still acts as a connector since it relates the meaning of one to the other.

Recognizing Subordination.   In each of the following sentences, identify the main clause by determining which clause contains the central idea. Underline the main clause once and the connecting word that links the clauses twice.

1. No one was killed because the avalanche occurred at night.
2. When silicon is added to iron, iron becomes rust resistant.
3. Even when heated to 1000° C, water will not decompose.
4. The gas pressure increased because the volume decreased.
5. When comets or meteors collided with the earth, the earth's magnetic field may have been reversed.
6. As the temperature increases, the rate of a chemical reaction increases.
7. Neon gives off light when an electric current is passed through it.
8. If carbon dioxide is cooled to $-79°$ C, it condenses directly to a solid.

Using Subordination.   In each of the following examples, combine the two clauses into one sentence so that one idea is subordinate to the other. You will need to add a connecting word such as *when, if, as, because,* or *so that.*

1. cause: mercury is heated to $-38.9°$ C
   effect: it melts

   When mercury is heated to $-38.9°$ C, it melts.

2. effect: no sound can be heard
   cause: a bell is struck in a vacuum
3. cause: chlorophyll disintegrates
   effect: leaves turn red, yellow, and orange
4. effect: an echo is heard
   cause: a sound wave reflects off a mountain
5. effect: ions are formed
   cause: an acid is dissolved in water
6. cause: a lens is too thin or an eyeball is too short
   effect: a person becomes farsighted

Recognizing Cause and Effect in a Paragraph.   Read the following description of an experiment and then answer the questions that follow.

STORED ENERGY

In a laboratory, chemistry students put some water into a beaker. They found the temperature of the water to be 19° C. Then they added pellets of sodium hydroxide to the water. To speed up the reaction, they stirred the pellets, causing them to break into sodium and hydroxide ions. When they were all dissolved, the students measured the temperature of the water again and found it to be 22° C. They thus learned that there is energy stored in the chemical bonds of sodium hydroxide. The breaking of those bonds resulted in the release of energy (3° C of heat), causing the temperature of the water to rise.

1. What caused the sodium hydroxide to break up?
2. What activity speeded up the reaction?
3. What caused the release of energy?
4. What caused the temperature of the water to rise?
5. What was the immediate effect of putting the sodium hydroxide pellets in water?
6. What was the effect of stirring the pellets?
7. What was the effect of breaking the bonds of sodium hydroxide?
8. What was the effect of the release of energy?

READING SKILLS

Vocabulary Building

An English word is formed from a root, which is its main part. Many words also contain prefixes, which come before the root, or suffixes, which follow the root, or both. (More than half of all commonly used English words are formed at least partly from Greek or Latin prefixes and roots.) Knowing the parts of a word can often be useful in determining its meaning. For example, knowing that the prefixes *un-*, *im-*, *in-*, *dis-* and *il-* make a word negative will tell you that *unnecessary* means *not necessary, impossible* means *not possible, inaccurate* means *not accurate, disconnected* means *not connected*, and *illogical* means *not logical*.

A word of caution is needed, however, for you cannot rely completely on such clues to determine meaning. English is a language that has evolved and changed over many years, absorbing words from many languages. The clues can sometimes be misleading. For example, *flammable* and *inflammable* have the same meaning! They both refer to something that can easily catch fire. (The antonym is *nonflammable* or *uninflammable*.) Therefore, you must always see if the meaning that you guessed fits the way the word is used in the sentence.

Prefixes: hyper-, hypo-, post-, sub-.   Study the following list of prefixes and then match the terms at the left below with their meanings at the right. You will not use all the meanings listed.

> *hyper-*: **over, above, beyond the norm;** *hypertension* = **high blood pressure**
>
> *hypo-*: **under, beneath, less than the norm;** *hypotension* = **low blood pressure**
>
> *post-*: **after;** *postglacial* = **after the glacial period**
>
> *sub-*: **under;** *submarine* = **a ship used under water**

_____*c*_____ 1. hypothermia   a. put under water

_____ 2. hypotoxic   b. less poisonous

_____ 3. hypoacidic   c. subnormal body temperature

_____ 4. hyperventilation   d. beneath the bottom of the sea

_____ 5. hypersonic   e. less acidic

_____ 6. postoperative   f. more acidic

_____ 7. postmortem   g. excessive breathing

_____ 8. submerge   h. highly poisonous

_____ 9. suboceanic   i. faster than the speed of sound

                                        j. after the operation

                                        k. after death

Vocabulary in Context.   Circle the letter of the answer that best matches the meaning of the italicized word as it is used in each of these sentences.

1. The best way to solve a problem is to find the *source*.
   (a.) origin   b. effects

2. Although he had no information, his *intuition* led to a solution of the problem.
   a. feeling   b. knowledge

3. The space between the earth and the moon is a *vacuum*.
   a. empty   b. full

4. The glass door was so *transparent*, we bumped into it.
   a. strong   b. clear

5. Fleming *revealed* that his discovery of penicillin was accidental.
   a. made known   b. kept hidden

6. The two paths *diverge* at the lake, as one goes north and the other goes east.
   a. come together   b. separate

7. The earth *absorbs* the water from the rain.
   a. drinks in   b. gives off

8. Wood is *opaque*; no light passes through it.
   a. unclear   b. clear

9. The *image* of the house was reflected in the water.
   a. picture   b. roof

10. The driver went in the *reverse* direction.
    a. identical   b. opposite

11. Air is the *medium* through which sound travels.
    a. process   b. environment

12. The old building was *transformed* into an emergency hospital.
    a. enlarged   b. changed

13. A microscope *magnifies* invisible objects so we can see them.
    a. enlarges   b. reduces

14. All efforts were *concentrated* on landing the plane safely.
    a. centered   b. scattered

Scanning

When you need to search technical material for the answers to specific questions, you will want to locate the particular information without reading every word. This can be accomplished by *scanning* the passage. To scan let your eyes run rapidly down the page and look for the key or important words that you are seeking.

Read the following three questions. Then find the answers by scanning the passage for the key words. Try to do it all in three minutes.

1. What is the speed of light? (key words: a large number)
2. Who originated the wave theory of light? (key words: a proper name with capital letters)
3. What is silver bromide used for? (key words: silver bromide)

Reading

Reflecting on Light

Most of what we know about the world comes to us through our ability to "see" with our eyes, our telescopes, and our microscopes. But how do we see? Sight is not something that reaches out *from* our eyes. Instead it is the light that travels *to* our eyes. You see this page, for example, because light, reflecting from the sun or an electric light, travels from the paper to your eyes.

Sometimes we see light as it comes from a direct source, such as the sun, fire, lightning, or a light bulb. The rest of the time we see light as it is reflected off objects.

Light travels at high speeds. It must have been a great leap in the intuition of scientists to realize that light actually ''travels.'' It isn't just there! In the air light travels at a speed of 186,000 miles per second. It travels slightly faster in a vacuum and slower in other transparent materials such as water or diamonds. It takes light less than one minute to travel from the earth to the moon and about 15 minutes to go from the earth to the sun.

In 1678 the Dutch scientist Christian Huygens was the first to propose that light travels in waves. Since then the work of the American Albert Einstein and the Scottish James Maxwell has revealed that light actually consists of particles known as photons and travels in electromagnetic waves. Light seems to travel in straight lines. If you shine a flashlight in the dark, for example, the beam of light appears to be straight. In contrast, sound waves travel in every direction. We can hear people on the other side of a wall but cannot see them.

In certain situations light diverges from a straight path. When it falls on an object, most is either absorbed (in the case of an opaque object such as wood or metal) or passes through (in the case of a transparent object such as water or glass). The remainder of the light is reflected. It is reflected light that changes direction. When light is reflected off a smooth surface, it changes direction in a regular way, that is, the angle that is reflected equals the angle at which it strikes the surface. If the surface is rough, light is reflected in many directions.

Light reflecting off a smooth surface.

Light reflecting off a rough surface.

Certain silver compounds (like silver bromide) reflect almost all the light that falls on them and are accordingly used for mirrors. The image that is reflected in a flat mirror is identical to the original object, even in size, except that the image is reversed. This is because light on a flat surface changes direction.

When light passes from one transparent medium to another, it changes speed and direction. This process, called refraction, explains the apparent shortening of a person's legs or the bending of a stick in water.

Light is a form of energy that can be transformed into heat. You can prove this by using a magnifying glass to concentrate the sun's rays on a piece of paper and

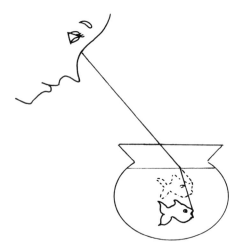

Light rays change direction in water.

burn a hole in it. It is this light energy from the sun that warms the earth and enables living things to grow. Plants get light energy directly from the sun. Animals get it from the plants they eat.

Making Inferences.   A scientist must make every effort to be precise by reading and observing carefully and measuring and recording accurately. Inaccurate information can result in incorrect conclusions. Indicate whether each of the following statements is stated in the passage (*S*), implied by other information in the passage (*I*), or neither stated nor implied (*N*). Do *not* indicate whether the statement is true or false.

_____*S*_____ 1. The speed of light is 186,000 miles per second.

_____ 2. Light travels slower through glass than through air.

_____ 3. Light travels faster than sound.

_____ 4. Moonlight is reflected light.

_____ 5. Light travels faster through water than sound does.

_____ 6. Scientists did not always know that light travels.

_____ 7. Light travels in the same way as sound.

_____ 8. Light travels at different speeds in different substances.

_____ 9. Sound waves do not travel in straight lines.

_____ 10. Most of the sound we hear is reflected.

_____ 11. Most of the sunlight falling on the tin roof of a building is absorbed.

_____ 12. An opaque object reflects more light than a transparent one.

_____ 13. A flat mirror reflects a reversed image.

_____ 14. Light energy can be converted to heat energy.

_____ 15. Scientists must be very clever people!

LISTENING SKILLS

Vocabulary in Context.   Circle the letter of the answer that best matches the meaning of the italicized word as it is used in each of these sentences.

1. Heavy machinery will produce *vibrations* that you can feel in the floor.
   a. noises   b. movement

2. In general, women's voices have a higher *pitch* than men's.
   a. sound   b. color

3. Sunglasses protect our eyes from the *intensity* of the sun's rays.
   a. strength   b. weakness

4. Tropical climates are characterized by a high *frequency* of rainfall.
   a. quality   b. recurrence

5. His poor health was *induced* by improper diet and smoking.
   a. prevented   b. caused

6. Because the *amplitude* of the universe is impossible for us to comprehend, we may never know how extensive it is.
   a. largeness   b. strangeness

7. Different wavelengths produce *variations* in colors.
   a. styles   b. differences

8. The *tone* of a violin is warm and rich.
   a. sound quality   b. price

9. To practice emergency procedures, we *simulated* an actual earthquake situation.
   a. observed   b. imitated

10. Tiny *acoustic* devices are used to aid hearing.
    a. visual   b. sound

11. Computers can be *programmed* to process and analyze all kinds of data.
    a. designed   b. destroyed

12. All theoretical research was suspended for the *duration* of the war.
    a. period   b. benefit

Note-Taking

When taking notes during a lecture, always focus on the main ideas. Listening for the main points is like looking for the topic sentences in a reading passage, although it is more difficult because you do not have paragraph clues to help you. You thus must listen for the general ideas or conclusions of the lecture.

Find out the topic or title of the lecture so you will have an idea of what it is going to cover and what you need to listen for. Sometimes the speaker states the objectives at the beginning of the presentation. Occasionally a speaker writes important points on a chalkboard or displays them on a slide or transparency. Finally, the speaker may summarize the main points of the lecture at the end.

Take notes as you listen to the lecture "The Music of Sound." Try to write down all the main ideas. Then use your notes to complete the next exercise.

Understanding the Lecture.   Use your notes to determine whether each of the following statements is true (*T*) or false (*F*) according to the lecture.

___*T*___ 1. Sound is produced by air vibrations.

_____ 2. Sound waves move in only one direction.

_____ 3. A bell rung in a vacuum will not produce a sound.

_____ 4. We hear sound when our ear drums vibrate and send messages to our brain.

_____ 5. Sound travels faster through the air than through the ground.

_____ 6. Pitch is determined by the size of sound waves.

_____ 7. A large drum produces a louder sound than a small one.

_____ 8. The amount of energy a sound wave is carrying is referred to as its amplitude.

_____ 9. A guitar sounds different from a clarinet because each instrument produces different combinations of vibrations.

_____ 10. A computer will never be able to simulate a human voice.

_____ 11. A computer can be programmed to play your favorite tune.

_____ 12. Computers will one day replace composers.

DISCUSSION POINTS

1. What are some of the beneficial effects of the technological advances in science in this century?
2. What are some of the harmful effects of modern technology?
3. What are some of the effects of space exploration?
4. What causes men and women to travel into space?
5. What might be the effects on earth of the discovery of life on another planet?
6. What are the possible effects of a continued expansion of world population?
7. What are some possible effects of a fuel shortage?
8. What are the effects of the computer on your life?

WRITING SKILLS

Patterns of Organization

When writing a paper, choose a logical order to present your information so that one idea leads to another. You might organize your paper according to one of the following concepts:
1. Time (chronology)
    a. For example, move from the initial effects of computers to the current effects to the possible future effects
2. Space
    a. For example, move from the effects of computers at home to the effects at your school to the effects at a work place such as a store, bank, or airline office
3. Logic
    a. Move from the general to the specific
        i. For example, move from the effects of computers on the world in general to the specific effects on one person
    b. Move from the specific to the general (the reverse of the above)
        i. For example, move from the specific effects of a fuel shortage on one person to the general effects on the world
    c. Move from the simple to the complex (never the reverse!)
        i. For example, move from the direct effects of computers to the indirect or secondary effects

Read the paragraph below and determine which of the above patterns of organization is used:

In 1954 a hydrogen bomb was tested at Bikini. The explosion produced the expected radio-active fall-out on a number of Pacific islands, and also scattered debris over thousands of square miles. As a result, dangerous radio-active materials appeared in the small plants which live in the surface of the sea; these were eaten by small animals which in turn were eaten by larger animals, notably the tuna fish which are an important article of diet in Japan. Hence a number of Japanese ingested quantities of radio-active food.

S. A. Barnett, *The Human Species:*
A Biology of Man (Harper & Row, 1971),
p. 208

In this paragraph, the effects of a hydrogen bomb test are described in chronological order because it is a chain reaction, that is, each effect in turn becomes the cause of another. These effects are introduced with the words *produced, as a result,* and *hence.* Other words that can introduce effects include *caused, induced, consequently, thus,* and *therefore.* Transition words that introduce causes include *is caused by, is produced by, is induced by, happens because,* and *is due to.*

Writing a Paragraph of Cause and Effect

Choose one scientific discovery or invention and write about its effects on your world. Or write about one of the Discussion Points. Use whatever pattern of organization (time, space, or logic) seems to work best for your topic, but be consistent throughout the paper. Start with a topic sentence that is broad enough to include everything you want to put in the paragraph.

chapter 4

Hypothesizing
Motion and Gravity

INTRODUCTION

When a scientist discovers a relationship that seems to hold true without exception, he or she formulates a *hypothesis*. A hypothesis is a tentative or temporary solution to a scientific problem or an explanation for why something happens. Although a hypothesis usually develops from the intuition of the scientist, it is based on observations or facts. For example, Charles Darwin's hypothesis about evolution came to him while he was riding in a carriage (he wrote, "I can remember the very spot in the road"), but the idea was the product of many years of study and experimentation.

A hypothesis does not always prove to be correct, and it may have to be rejected altogether or at least revised. Progress involves continually refining hypotheses as new information comes to light. For example, since no one has ever seen the structure of an atom, scientists continually revise their hypothesis about what it looks like.

As evidence is gathered to support a hypothesis and it becomes accepted in the scientific world, it is referred to as a *theory* (for example, the theory of relativity). When a theory explains or unifies a great deal of information, it becomes known as a *principle*, or *natural law* (for example, Archimedes' principle of water displacement or the law of gravity).

Short Reading

Read the passage below and find Aristotle's and Galileo's hypotheses about motion.

Some Notions About Motion

Which falls faster, a blade of grass or a stone? Anyone can see that a stone falls faster. And that is what the ancient Greeks believed. Based on everyday experience, Aristotle determined that heavy objects fall faster than light objects and that objects fall with a speed proportional to their weight.

Aristotle also studied horizontal motion. He observed that whenever he pushed a rock or other object, it always rolled for a while and then came to rest. He hypothesized that the natural state of an object is to be at rest and a force is necessary to keep an object in motion. Aristotle's hypotheses were accepted for two thousand years because they were consistent with logic and informal observation.

It was not until the early 1600s that these long-established beliefs were challenged. Galileo was not content to accept ideas without verifying them with experiments. He dropped various weights from a height and recorded the results. Disproving Aristotle's hypothesis, he determined that all bodies fall at equal rates, if you discount the air resistance. A blade of grass will fall more slowly than a stone only because it meets with more resistance from the air.

Galileo also disproved Aristotle's hypothesis about horizontal motion. He demonstrated that a body pushed on a smooth surface could go much further than one pushed on a rough surface. When a lubricant such as oil was used, almost no force was required to keep the object in motion. He concluded that if an object does not meet with resistance (friction), it will continue to move at a constant speed even if no force is applied.

Half a century later, Newton extended Galileo's ideas and formulated a theory that a body at rest will remain at rest and a body in motion will remain in motion unless some outside force acts on it. This theory is so universally accepted it is referred to as Newton's first law of motion.

USING ENGLISH TO HYPOTHESIZE

A hypothesis is a tentative proposition that resolves a problem or answers a scientific question. A theory is a hypothesis that is generally accepted. However, the words *hypothesis* and *theory* are frequently used interchangeably.

The following are examples of hypotheses from the reading:

Aristotle's hypotheses: **Objects fall with a speed proportional to their weight.**

The natural state of an object is to be at rest and a force is necessary to keep an object in motion.

Note that although it may appear within a sentence, the hypothesis itself is always in the form of a complete sentence, *not* a sentence fragment or a question.

Galileo's hypotheses: **All bodies fall at equal rates.**

If an object does not meet with resistance, it will continue to move at a constant speed even if no force is applied.

Most hypotheses are stated in the present simple tense, although it is possible to hypothesize about something that happened in the past or will happen in the future. Sometimes a hypothesis is expressed as a prediction, using the future tense with *will*. The meaning is the same as if the present tense were used. Saying something always happens is the same as predicting that it will happen.

Identifying Hypotheses in Sentences.   Circle a or b in each of these pairs of sentences to indicate the one that can be considered a hypothesis.

1. a. Migration is the seasonal movement of animals from one place to another.
    (b.) Birds may be guided in their migration by the position of the sun or stars.

2. a. Rocks fall faster than feathers.
    b. There may be a fifth force in nature that causes objects to fall at different rates.

3. a. Certain types of music may relieve stress.
    b. During the Middle Ages, music was used to treat certain diseases, such as the plague.

4. a. Language is thought to be a function of the left side of the brain.
    b. The largest part of the brain is the cerebrum.

5. a. The Big Bang theory was first proposed by a Belgian mathematician, Abbé Georges Lemaître, in 1927.
    b. The universe was born about 18 billion years ago when a cosmic egg, containing all the matter and energy existing in the universe today, exploded into millions of pieces.

6. a. Some elephants, whales, dolphins, and porpoises have brains larger than the human brain.
    b. Dinosaurs may have become extinct because their brains were not proportional to their brawn.

7. a. Excessive amounts of cholesterol might cause heart attacks.
    b. Eggs, cheese, and fatty meats all contain cholesterol.

Identifying a Hypothesis in a Paragraph.   Underline the hypothesis or theory in the following paragraph.

WHAT TIME IS IT?

Suppose a football game begins at 1:00 P.M. in New York City. It is then 10:00 A.M. in Los Angeles and 6:00 P.M. in London. Which time is correct? If an explosion occurred on a star, scientists on the earth would register the time it happened. But anyone traveling in another part of the universe in a different direction would identify the time differently. Thus time, like space and motion, is relative; there is no real or absolute time. This concept was brought to the attention of the world by Albert Einstein in 1905.

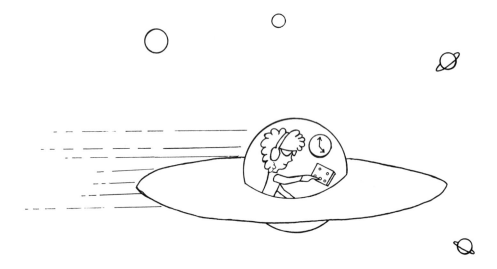

Probability

Hypotheses are often expressed with words that indicate their tentative nature or unproven status. These words are very important. To say "there is life on Jupiter" is entirely different from saying "there may be life on Jupiter." In the following list, the first sentence expresses probability most strongly and each succeeding sentence expresses it slightly less strongly.

> **There is life on Jupiter.**
> **There must be life on Jupiter.**
> **There is probably life on Jupiter.**
> **There may be life on Jupiter.**
> **There could be life on Jupiter.**
> **There might be life on Jupiter.**
> **It is unlikely that there is life on Jupiter.**
> **It is impossible for there to be life on Jupiter.**
> **There is no life on Jupiter.**

Identifying Probability.   There are many ways to express probability. Circle the word or words that indicate probability in each of these sentences.

1. Light (seems) to travel in waves.

2. The accumulation of carbon dioxide in the air is believed to be warming the earth to a dangerous level.

3. Pulsars are thought by some scientists to be rapidly spinning neutron stars.

4. Current research suggests that obesity is hereditary.

5. The universe appears to be expanding.

6. As far as we know, the earth is 4.6 billion years old.

7. It is possible that the universe is expanding and contracting in some rhythmic way.

8. Theoretically, computers will be able to design and create in ways that are undreamed of today.

Using Modals of Probability. Modals are a group of auxiliary verbs that modify verbs. Probability may be expressed with the use of the modals *must, may, might,* and *could.* The modal *must* conveys a much stronger probability than the others. In scientific writing, these modals are frequently used with the verb *to be.* Formulate sentences with either *must be, may be, might be,* or *could be* following the pattern of the first pair of sentences below.

1. Is the "greenhouse effect" warming our earth?

    The "greenhouse effect" may be warming our earth.

2. Are the pandas in China becoming extinct?
3. Are the ocean's tides slowing the rotation of the earth?
4. Are quasars violently exploding galaxies?
5. Are the continents drifting or moving on the surface of the earth?
6. Is the radioactive fallout from nuclear test explosions harmful to the atmosphere?
7. Is the population of the world increasing at a dangerous rate?
8. Are computers revolutionizing industry around the world?

READING SKILLS

Vocabulary Building

A knowledge of prefixes and other word parts will not only help you identify new words but also greatly expand your vocabulary. Just knowing that the prefix *re-* means *again* can vastly increase the number of verbs you know. For example, *re-* + *write* = *rewrite* (meaning *to write again*). Similarly, *re-* may be added to many other English verbs to form new verbs. Examples include *recalculate, readmit, re-release, reproduce, reenter, reactivate, recharge, reorganize, reappear, redirect, reapply, reexamine,* and *retest.*

However, a warning is necessary for students of English as a second language. Many English words begin with the letters *re* but not the prefix *re-*, such as: *resource, revolve, reject, reflect, resist, refuse, reserve, resemble, reveal, refer,* and *reduce.* Interestingly, although there are many such verbs, they often contain the meaning of *again* or a repeated action, as is true of *renew, repeat, review, revive, return, remember,* and *reciprocate.*

Prefix: trans-.   Study the following prefix and then complete the sentences below, using a dictionary if necessary.

trans-: over, across, beyond, through

translucent—allowing light to pass through

1. Metal and wood are opaque; glass and water are *trans*parent_____.

2. Maria does not speak English, so you will have to *trans*_____ for her.

3. The hospital patient received a blood *trans*_____.

4. A *trans*_____ in a radio amplifies the signal without using a vacuum tube.

5. Sound is *trans*_____ in waves; it cannot travel through a vacuum.

6. The professor *trans*_____ to another university in his hometown.

7. Many lives are saved by kidney and liver *trans*_____ from one person to another.

8. Light energy can be *trans*_____ into heat energy.

Vocabulary in Context.   Circle the letter of the answer that best matches the meaning of the italicized word as it is used in each of these sentences.

1. The results of the experiment *verified* that our theory was correct.
   a. disproved   (b.) proved

2. The lesson was *extended* one hour to allow time for questions.
   a. lengthened   b. shortened

3. The *horizontal* lines on the map indicate east-west routes.
   a. side-to-side   b. up-and-down

4. The structure is resting on four *vertical* posts.
   a. level   b. up-and-down

5. His *inertia* was caused by hot weather and fatigue.
   a. activity   b. inactivity

6. The truck *accelerated* when it started downhill.
   a. slowed down   b. speeded up

7. The automobile tires were worn out by *friction*.
   a. age   b. rubbing

8. Europe and Asia make up the largest land *mass* on earth.
   a. ocean   b. body

9. The students' names were listed in *inverse* alphabetical order.
   a. correct   b. reverse

10. The *proportion* of hydrogen to oxygen in water is 2 to 1.
    a. relationship   b. distance

11. The researchers were pleased because the results of the experiment *were consistent* with their expectations.
    a. agreed   b. disagreed

12. The football game was a good match because the two teams were *balanced*.
    a. equal   b. strong

13. The design of the Taj Mahal in India is *symmetrical*; all sides are equal.
    a. regular   b. irregular

14. We had to rest after *exerting* all our energy to push the car up the hill.
    a. using   b. saving

15. Automobiles *expel* carbon monoxide, which pollutes the air.
    a. give off   b. absorb

16. The wind *propelled* the sailboat along the water.
    a. pulled   b. pushed

17. The humidity *altered* the results of the experiment and we had to redo it.
    a. changed   b. improved

18. Water can be formed by the *synthesis* of hydrogen and oxygen.
    a. separation   b. combination

19. It is *logical* to assume that the next century will be more advanced technologically than this one.
    a. unreasonable   b. reasonable

Finding Main Ideas

A good way to read any textbook is to bracket or highlight the topic sentence of each paragraph or section. Later, to review the material for a test, you only need to read the topic sentences for a summary of all the main points.

Reading

Put square brackets around the topic sentence of every paragraph in the following passage. Note that here the topic sentences are usually found toward the ends of the paragraphs because the information builds up to a conclusion.

Newton Explains Motion

[Although many scientists studied motion, it was the great Sir Isaac Newton who formulated the theories of motion, verifying and extending the earlier work of Galileo and Copernicus.] Newton studied horizontal and vertical motion.

First Newton studied the quality of inertia, or the tendency of a body to resist change in its state of motion or direction. A tennis ball, for example, has little inertia; it is easy to get it to move, stop, or change direction. A truck, on the other hand, has a great deal of inertia. Newton concluded that a body at rest will remain at rest and that a body in motion will remain in motion unless some outside force acts on it. This principle is called the law of inertia, or Newton's first law of motion.

But Newton's curiosity was not satisfied. He wondered what causes a change in motion. Why does a body at rest begin to move or a body in motion change its direction? He determined that if a body is at rest, no force is acting on it; however, when a force acts on a body, the force will speed up, slow down, or change the direction of that body.

Moreover, Newton discovered that there is a relationship between force and acceleration. If you push a swing gently, it will move slowly. If you push it harder, it will go faster. Newton noted that if you discount the friction involved, the amount of force is directly related to the amount of acceleration.

The acceleration is also related to the mass of the object. Mass, which is the quantity of matter in a body, also determines the amount of inertia an object has. A truck has a great deal of mass, a bicycle has much less. If you use an equal amount of force to push a bicycle and a truck, the bicycle will go much faster than the truck. The larger the mass, the less the acceleration. In fact, the acceleration of a body is inversely proportional to its mass. Newton's second law of motion states that the acceleration of a body is directly related to the force acting on it and inversely proportional to its mass. The direction of the acceleration is in the direction of the applied force.

Finally, Newton explored the question of the source of force. He observed that the force acting on a body comes from another body. But this idea by itself was not consistent with his view of a balanced and symmetrical universe. He therefore concluded that whenever there is a force pushing in one direction, there is another

When you push a wall, it exerts an equal and opposite force on you.

force pushing back. This concept may be difficult to imagine, but try pulling on a rubber band and you will feel it pulling back on you. Also notice what happens to your finger when you press it against a table. Objects can exert a force because all materials are elastic to some extent, although the elasticity of walls and tables may be slight. When you push off against the wall of a swimming pool, for example, you start to move away from the wall. The wall is exerting a force on you that causes you to move in the opposite direction. And if you think the floor does not push back against your feet, why do your shoes wear out, and why do your feet hurt you after you have been on them for a long time? Why do automobile tires wear out? Thus Newton stated his third law: whenever one object exerts a force on a second object, the second object exerts an equal and opposite force on the first.

The movement of a rocket is also based on this law. The rocket expels gases, which then exert an equal and opposite force propelling the rocket forward. In space, a vehicle can alter its speed or direction by expelling rockets in the opposite direction.

Newton's laws are applicable everywhere in the universe and synthesize both vertical and horizontal motion. The concept that the universe functions according to logical, orderly natural laws influenced not only the scientific world but also the social, political, and philosophical thinking of the Western world for two hundred years.

Understanding the Reading.   Indicate whether each of the following sentences is true (*T*) or false (*F*) according to the information in the passage above.

_____*F*_____ 1. Although many scientists studied motion, Newton was the first.

_____ 2. Galileo's ideas were based on Newton's work.

_____ 3. Newton's third law is the law of inertia.

_____ 4. Inertia is the tendency of a body to resist change.

_____   5. Any change in motion is produced by a force.

_____   6. Acceleration is proportional to mass.

_____   7. The direction of acceleration is opposite to the direction of force.

_____   8. Pushing off against the side of a swimming pool is an example of Newton's second law.

_____   9. Newton believed that the universe is symmetrical and balanced.

_____ 10. Every action produces an equal and opposite reaction.

_____ 11. A rocket functions on the principle of action and reaction.

_____ 12. According to Newton, your shoes wear out because you are wearing the wrong brand.

_____ 13. Newton's ideas influenced world thinking in fields other than science.

LISTENING SKILLS

Vocabulary in Context.   Circle the letter of the answer that best matches the meaning of the italicized word as it is used in each of these sentences.

1. Gravity keeps the moon in its *orbit* around the earth.
   a. path   b. position

2. Scientists are still *speculating* about the origin of the universe.
   a. thinking   b. experimenting

3. Objects fall downward because of the earth's *gravity*.
   a. pull   b. movement

4. The professor was always on time and began the lecture *precisely* at noon.
   a. approximately   b. exactly

5. Your weight *varies* from day to day.
   a. changes   b. increases

6. Astronauts experience *weightlessness* when traveling in space.
   a. no weight   b. heaviness

7. The *relative* advantages of copper and silver wire were studied and compared.
   a. comparative   b. important

8. Newton *calculated* the size of the planets.
   a. computed   b. reported

9. The *tide* washed the sea shells from the beach.
   a. ocean current   b. sand

10. There is a *correlation* between heredity and certain diseases, like hemophilia.
    a. connection   b. difference

11. We see the moon in different *phases*, such as the quarter-moon and half-moon.
    a. stages   b. places

Note-Taking

Taking notes is a challenging task. The chief problem is that while you are writing, the instructor is still talking and may be making important points that you are missing. Even a native speaker cannot listen to one thing and write something else at the same time while concentrating on both.

Therefore, you must write quickly. One good way to do this is to use shortened forms of long words as well as symbols and abbreviations. It is *not* necessary to know standard abbreviations. You may use your own as long as you can write them quickly and read them back later. The following hints may help:

1. Write only the first part of a long word.

scientific knowledge	**sci knowl**
chemically active	**chem act**
atmospheric pressure	**atmos press**

2. Use symbols and abbreviations.

Malleable and ductile	**mall & duct**
one gram	**1 gm**
ninety percent	**90%**
mix with water	**mix w/H$_2$O**

Note: Only use shortened forms of words you are familiar with! If a word is new, write it out.

Take notes as you listen to the lecture "Obeying the Law of Gravity," and then use your notes to complete the next exercise.

Understanding the Lecture.   Indicate whether each of the following sentences is true (*T*) or false (*F*) according to the information in the lecture.

___*F*___   1. Newton demonstrated that movement on the earth is different from movement in the heavens.

_____ 2. Planets are held in their orbits by the force of gravity.

_____ 3. Your mass would be different on Mars.

_____ 4. Astronauts weigh less on the moon because there are no good restaurants there.

_____ 5. Astronauts experience weightlessness while traveling in space because they are too far from the gravitational pull of the earth or the moon.

_____ 6. Newton calculated the relative weights of the planets by studying their gravitational pull.

_____ 7. There is a stronger force of attraction between the sun and the earth than between the earth and the moon.

_____ 8. The ocean's tides are caused by eclipses.

_____ 9. You cannot feel the gravitational pull between yourself and the person sitting next to you because it is so weak.

_____ 10. The law of gravity is universal and applies everywhere.

DISCUSSION POINTS

1. Form a hypothesis to explain why some students succeed in their school work while others, with equal ability, fail.
2. Form a hypothesis to explain why some students experiment with drugs.
3. Form a hypothesis to explain why some students drop out of school.
4. Form a hypothesis to explain why some people do not wear seat belts in their cars.
5. Form a hypothesis to explain why many drivers go faster than the speed limit.
6. Form a hypothesis to explain why some students, although honest in other ways, will cheat on a test.
7. Form a hypothesis to explain why some students seem to make friends easily, while others do not.

WRITING SKILLS

Writing Conclusions

A short paragraph does not require a concluding statement, but a longer paper should have a conclusion instead of just ending abruptly. A conclusion is important because it is the final thought given to the reader and thus has the strongest impact. Therefore, the conclusion should contain whatever you want the reader to re-member. A concluding sentence may do one of the following:

1. Restate the main point for emphasis. This involves paraphrasing or rewriting the topic sentence.
2. Summarize the information to review or clarify it. In a short paper, a summary may not be different from the main point.
3. Relate the significance of what was written. Why is it important? What effect will it have? What can be done about it? What should the reader do?

Transition words for writing a conclusion include *therefore, as a result, for this reason, thus, hence, consequently, so, because of this,* and *for this reason.*

Writing a Paragraph with a Conclusion

Write a paragraph based on one of the hypotheses formulated in the Discussion Points. The hypothesis is your topic sentence. The rest of the paragraph should support the hypothesis, that is, give reasons for your opinion. Finally, write a concluding statement that relates the significance of what you have written.

For example, suppose you state in your paper that students who have set their professional goals do better in school than those who have not. Your conclusion might be that schools should require students to state their major before they are admitted. Or you might suggest that this subject needs further research. Suppose your hypothesis is that students take drugs because of peer pressure. You might conclude that we need to change the attitude of young people toward drugs.

Be sure that your concluding statement answers *one* of these questions:

1. Why is your hypothesis important?
2. What effect will it have?
3. What can be done about it?
4. What should the reader do?

chapter 5

Defining
Energy

INTRODUCTION

When making a hypothesis or other statement, scientists must make sure they are understood by other researchers. Misunderstandings occur when there are different concepts of what is being discussed.

A definition answers the question, "What is it?" Sometimes a definition is necessary because a word or concept has more than one meaning. For example, whether carbon is a metal or nonmetal depends on how you define carbon. At other times, a definition is required because a term is being used in a special way. For example, physicists use the terms *work* and *energy* in ways that are more specific than their common meanings. A definition should be complete enough to include all the items in the category yet narrow enough to eliminate items that do not belong. The Greek philosopher Plato once defined man as a two-legged creature that has no feathers. His critic Diogenes left the room and brought back a bird without feathers, declaring, "Here is Plato's man!" The problem with Plato's definition was that it did not distinguish a man from other two-legged creatures without feathers. Communication between researchers is dependent on precise definitions of substances, concepts, processes, and ideas.

Short Reading

Read the following passage to find definitions for as many types of energy as you can.

The Many Forms of Energy

Energy is the ability to do work. When a hammer strikes a nail, it exerts a force on the nail that causes it to move. The movement of the hammer has the ability to do work and therefore has a form of energy that we call kinetic energy. Kinetic energy is the energy of motion.

An object may have energy not only because of its motion but also because of its position or shape. For example, when a watch spring is wound, it is storing energy. When this energy is released, it will do the work of moving the hands of the watch. This form of energy is called potential energy. Potential energy is stored energy. Water in a dam is another example of potential energy.

There are many types of kinetic and potential energy, including chemical, thermal, mechanical, electrical, and nuclear energy. Chemical energy is potential energy that is stored in gasoline, food, and oil. Just as the watch spring needs to be released to do the work of moving the hands, the energy stored in food molecules needs to be released by enzymes or substances in the body, and the energy stored in gasoline must be released by the spark plug to do its work of propelling the car forward. Thermal energy may be defined as the kinetic energy of molecules. When a substance is heated, the molecules move faster, which causes that substance to feel hot. Mechanical energy is energy related to the movement of objects. Electric energy is energy that is produced by electric charges. Nuclear energy is the energy that is stored in the nucleus of certain kinds of atoms, like uranium.

USING ENGLISH TO DEFINE

Aristotle suggested that a good definition should include the general classification of a term plus the specific characteristics that differentiate the term from other members of its class. For example, a definition of a giraffe should include a classification, such as, *A giraffe is an animal*, and specific characteristics, such as, *A giraffe is a tall, African animal with a very long neck.*

Definition formula:

Term = Class + Characteristics

Chemical energy is potential energy that is stored in gasoline, food, and oil.
(Frequently, the characteristics appear as a relative clause beginning with *which, that, who,* or *where.*)

TERM		CLASS		CHARACTERISTICS
chemical energy	=	potential energy	+	that is stored in gasoline, food, and oil

Mechanical energy is energy related to the movement of objects.
(The characteristics sometimes appear as a relative clause in which *which, that, who,* or *where* has been deleted.)

TERM		CLASS		CHARACTERISTICS
mechanical energy	=	energy	+	(that is) related to the movement of objects

Energy is the ability to do work. . . . Kinetic energy is the energy of motion.
(Sometimes the characteristics take the form of an infinitive phrase or prepositional phrase.)

TERM		CLASS		CHARACTERISTICS
energy	=	ability	+	to do work INFINITIVE PHRASE
kinetic energy	=	energy	+	of motion PREPOSITIONAL PHRASE

Thermal energy may be defined as the kinetic energy of molecules.
(The use of the modal of possibility *may* indicates that there is more than one way to define something.)

TERM		CLASS		CHARACTERISTICS
thermal energy	=	**kinetic energy**	+	**of molecules**

Potential energy is stored energy.
(Sometimes the characteristics precede the class.)

TERM		CHARACTERISTIC		CLASS
potential energy	=	**stored**	+	**energy**

NOTE: When defining, remember the following:
1. Definitions require the present simple tense and the verb *to be*.
2. The definite article, *the,* is usually not used with the term being defined because definitions are general statements. For example, we would define *a* giraffe (in general), not *the* giraffe (a specific giraffe).

Sentence Patterns

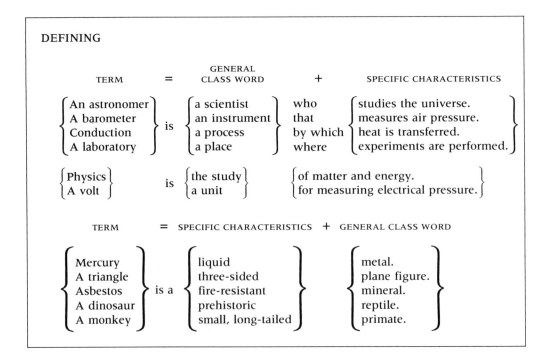

DEFINING

TERM	=	GENERAL CLASS WORD	+	SPECIFIC CHARACTERISTICS
An astronomer		a scientist	who	studies the universe.
A barometer	is	an instrument	that	measures air pressure.
Conduction		a process	by which	heat is transferred.
A laboratory		a place	where	experiments are performed.
Physics	is	the study		of matter and energy.
A volt		a unit		for measuring electrical pressure.

TERM	=	SPECIFIC CHARACTERISTICS	+	GENERAL CLASS WORD
Mercury		liquid		metal.
A triangle		three-sided		plane figure.
Asbestos	is a	fire-resistant		mineral.
A dinosaur		prehistoric		reptile.
A monkey		small, long-tailed		primate.

Analyzing Definitions.   In each of the following definitions, underline the general class once, and the specific characteristic(s) twice.

1. Helium is an inert gas that is light and nonflammable.

2. Protozoa are one-celled organisms.

3. A machine is a device that transforms energy from one form to another.

4. The cerebrum is the part of the brain that is the center of reasoning.

5. An insulator is a substance that does not conduct heat or electricity.

6. Fog is a cloud that forms on the ground.

7. Ecology is the study of the environment.

8. A satellite is a celestial body that orbits another celestial body.

Correcting Definitions.   Listed in the box are some guidelines for writing good definitions and following are some poorly written definitions. Determine what is wrong with each definition and discuss how you would improve it.

- Identify the class. Examples, descriptions, or comparisons may be included in your definition, but they should not replace the class term.

- Be precise. Saying that "carbon dioxide is a gas" is not enough. What are the specific characteristics that differentiate it from other gases?

- Beware of circular definitions. A statement like "an agronomist is a person who practices agronomy" clarifies nothing.

- Make sure the definition is not more difficult than the term you are defining. A definition should clarify, not confuse.

- Use negative definitions like "a tomato is not a vegetable," when you think people have a wrong idea. But then follow it with a proper definition. Now that we know what it isn't, what is it?

- Be objective. Saying that "a pizza is something really good to eat" explains nothing to a Martian who has never seen a pizza.

---

1. A scientific theory is a theory like Darwin's theory.
2. An apple is round, red, and about the size of a fist.
3. Calculus is a tough subject.
4. An ear is an auditory appendage of *Homo sapiens* and other species.
5. A unicorn is not a real animal.
6. Tornadoes are very dangerous.
7. Radium is an element.

8. A compass looks like a clock.
9. An amphibian is like a frog or a turtle.
10. A supernova is a big nova.

Relative Clauses

A clause is a part of a sentence that contains a noun and a verb. A relative clause is one that begins with *which, that, where,* or *who. Which* and *that* are most commonly used in science definitions; *who* is used when referring to people. Science definitions often include relative clauses containing the characteristics that distinguish an item from others in the class.

Using Relative Clauses.   Combine each of the following pairs of sentences to produce a one-sentence definition with a relative clause.

1. Protons are positively charged particles. They are contained in the nucleus of an atom.

   Protons are positively charged particles that are contained in the nucleus of an atom.

2. A black hole is an area in space. It has a gravitational pull so powerful that nothing, not even light, can escape.
3. Marine biologists are scientists. They study animals and plants that live in the sea.
4. The stratosphere is a portion of the atmosphere. It is over seven miles high.
5. Insulin is used in the treatment of diabetes. It is a hormone produced by the pancreas.
6. The most abundant form of life on earth are bacteria. They are simple forms of plant life.
7. Oxidation is a chemical reaction. It involves the loss of one or more electrons by an atom or ion.
8. Nitrogen makes up 80 percent of the air. It is a colorless, odorless gas.

Formulating Definitions.   Using the information given in each series, write a definition. Use the sentence patterns at the beginning of this unit to guide you.

1. an amoeba / one-celled animal / constantly changes its shape

   An amoeba is a one-celled animal that constantly changes its shape.

2. an antibiotic / drug / cures bacterial diseases
3. lung / organ / breathing

4. acoustics / science / sound
5. photosynthesis / process / plants manufacture food
6. catalyst / substance / speeds up but is not changed by a chemical reaction
7. calorie / unit / measures heat
8. cyclotron / apparatus / bombards the nuclei of atoms

Creating Definitions.   A good way to see if a definition is complete is to reverse it. For example, if we reverse *an elephant is an animal*, we get *an animal is an elephant*, and it is obvious that the definition is inadequate. Formulate a definition for each of the following words and test each one by reversing it. If you need help, use a dictionary.

1. a camera
2. a bridge
3. an x-ray
4. a butterfly
5. geology

6. a diamond
7. an echo
8. a virus
9. caffeine
10. an aquarium

An elephant is an animal with big ears and a trunk.

READING SKILLS

Vocabulary Building

One way to guess the meaning of a new word is to see if it is related to one you already know. For example, if you already know the meaning of *benefit*, you can guess that the word *beneficial* refers to something good. Related words also help you to remember a new word. For example, if you know that *toxic* means poisonous, it will be easy to remember that *intoxicated* means poisoned with drugs or alcohol. And if you know that the *horizon* is the line where the sky seems to meet the earth, you will remember that a *horizontal line* goes from side to side rather than up and down.

However, just as word parts can sometimes be misleading, related words can occasionally lead you astray. For example, although *infinite* means enormous or very large, *infinitesimal* means tiny or very small! The only way to guard against making mistakes is to see if the meaning you have guessed fits the sentence and paragraph.

Prefixes: **ecto-/exo-, endo-, micro-, macro-.** Study the following list of prefixes and then match the terms at the left below with their meanings at the right. You will not use all the meanings listed.

    ecto- **or** *exo-*: **outside**
        exogenous—**due to external causes**

    endo-: **inside**
        endogenous—**due to internal causes**

    micro-: **small**
        microscopic—**too small to be seen without a microscope**

    macro-: **large**
        macroscopic—**large enough to be seen with the naked eye**

_d_ 1. ectoplasm

_____ 2. endoplasm

_____ 3. microbe

_____ 4. microcosm

_____ 5. micrometer

_____ 6. microthermal

_____ 7. microsecond

_____ 8. macronucleus

_____ 9. macrocosm

a. the entire universe

b. a little universe

c. a minute period of time

d. external layer of protoplasm

e. internal layer of protoplasm

f. a very minute organism

g. relating to small quantities of heat

h. a large, dense nucleus

i. an instrument for measuring distances or angles

j. a minute cell

Vocabulary in Context.   Circle the letter of the answer that best matches the meaning of the italicized word as it is used in each of these sentences.

1. Frayed electrical wires are *potential* fire hazards.
   (a.) probable   b. unlikely

2. The *velocity* of the wind increased during the storm.
   a. sound   b. speed

3. Despite the head-on collision, the engine remained *intact*.
   a. whole   b. broken

4. The *conservation* of natural resources, such as rivers and forests, is an important issue of our time.
   a. preservation   b. observation

5. When the temperature dropped, *vapor* accumulated on the inside of the window.
   a. steam   b. dust

6. Pasteur's germ theory proved to be *valid* and was a major breakthrough in the history of medicine.
   a. false   b. true

7. When the bottle was uncapped, all the pressure inside was *released*.
   a. set free   b. increased

8. Energy is released by the *fission* of atomic nuclei.
   a. splitting   b. combining

9. The cold on top of the mountain got more *intense* later in the evening.
   a. extreme   b. moderate

10. An alloy is a *fusion* of two or more metals that makes a stronger metal.
    a. combination   b. separation

Scanning

Scan the following passage in three minutes or less and put brackets around the following:

1. A definition of *work* (key words: work, defined)
2. The name of the French chemist who studied chemical changes in 1785 (key words: 1785, French—look for a capital *F*)
3. The meaning of the letter *c* in the equation $E = mc^2$ (key words: $E = mc^2$, the letter *c*)

Reading

$$E = mc^2$$

Energy can be transformed or changed from one type to another. For example, an apple hanging on a tree has potential energy, or the energy of position. As it falls, it loses potential energy because its height decreases. At the same time, it gains kinetic energy, or the energy of motion, because its velocity increases. Potential energy is being transformed into kinetic energy.

Frequently, the transfer of energy involves a transfer from one body to another. When you lift up a rock, you are changing the chemical energy of the food you have eaten into muscle energy. As you lift the rock high, your muscle energy is changing into the rock's potential energy.

Muscle energy is transformed into mechanical energy.

When energy is transformed from one type to another or transferred from one body to another, no energy is lost. When we measure energy, we discover that the total amount remains intact. Suppose we prepared, cooked, and then ate some food. If we were to measure carefully all the energy that remains at the end of this process (such as potential, kinetic, and heat), we would always find exactly the same amount of energy as we started with (such as chemical and potential). Energy can thus be converted from one form to another but never created or destroyed. This is called the law of the conservation of energy.

Matter, like energy, can be converted from one form to another but neither be created nor destroyed. In 1785, the French chemist Antoine Lavoisier demonstrated that there is no gain or loss of mass in a chemical change. For example, when a piece of wood is burned, ashes remain. At the same time, the wood combines with oxygen in the air to form carbon dioxide and water vapor, which pass into the air. If the carbon dioxide, water vapor, and ashes are added together, the total weight will equal the original weight of the wood plus the oxygen in the air. Thus, there is no change in the total mass. This is called the law of the conservation of mass.

Many years later, Albert Einstein theorized that the conservation of energy is not distinct from the conservation of mass, that is, that there is a single law, the law of conservation of matter and energy. He predicted that matter could be changed into energy and vice versa. This concept was expressed in his famous equation $E = mc^2$, where E represents the amount of energy, m is the amount of matter, and c is a constant equal to the speed of light.

Einstein's theory proved to be valid in 1939, when it was discovered that enormous amounts of energy could be released by splitting uranium atoms, a process called fission. When a uranium or plutonium atom is split apart, it gives up neutrons that in turn split other atoms. This chain reaction takes place very rapidly and releases a huge amount of energy, resulting in the explosion of an atomic bomb.

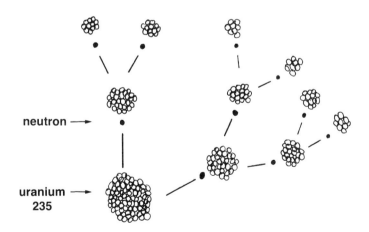

neutron →

uranium
235 →

Nuclear chain reaction.

Although it may seem strange, a process that is the exact opposite of fission can also release great quantities of energy. Under conditions of intense heat, such as are found at the center of the sun, hydrogen atoms combine to form helium atoms. The transformation of hydrogen into helium is called fusion. When fusion takes place, the hydrogen atoms lose a small amount of mass, which is transferred into energy. Fusion produced on the earth results in a hydrogen bomb, which is much more powerful than the original atomic bomb. But the principle of fusion can also be used to produce energy for peaceful purposes that can supply all of the needs of the human race for a long time.

Understanding the Reading.   Each of the following statements is inconsistent with the information in the previous passage. Test your reading comprehension by finding the error in each statement and restating it correctly.

1. Energy can be transformed from one type to another, but it cannot be transferred from one body to another.

   Energy can be transformed from one type to another or transferred from one body to another.

2. Kinetic energy is the energy of position.
3. Unlike matter, energy cannot be created or destroyed.
4. Potential energy is when you lie in bed thinking of all the things you have to do.
5. Einstein said that the conservation of matter and the conservation of energy are unrelated.
6. Einstein's theory about the conservation of matter and energy was never proved.
7. The development of atomic energy demonstrates that energy can be converted into matter.
8. When an atom is split, it gives off electrons.
9. An atomic explosion occurs as a result of the slow chain reaction of splitting atoms.
10. Fusion takes place on the sun when two uranium atoms are combined.
11. Extreme heat or cold is required for fusion to take place.
12. Fusion produced on the earth results in an atomic explosion.

LISTENING SKILLS

Vocabulary in Context.   Circle the letter of the answer that best matches the meaning of the italicized word as it is used in each of these sentences.

1. Scientists do not *assume* something is true until evidence confirms it.
   a. accept   b. deny

2. It was once thought our natural resources were *inexhaustible*.
   a. limited
   b. endless

3. When we use energy, we *degrade* that energy to a less useful form.
   a. reduce
   b. improve

4. His sickness was *manifested* by pain and fever.
   a. indicated
   b. cured

5. Despite setbacks, they *proceeded* with the experiment.
   a. went forward
   b. went backward

6. Ice is water in its solid *state*.
   a. process
   b. condition

7. We could not find the papers because the laboratory was *in disorder*.
   a. organized
   b. disorganized

8. The condition of the patient has *degenerated* despite the operation.
   a. worsened
   b. improved

9. If fuel is not conserved, our resources may one day be *depleted*.
   a. used up
   b. saved

Note-Taking

Since speed is important in note-taking, do not try to write in perfect sentences or correct grammar. Keep in mind that no one is going to see your notes except you. Just make sure that they are clear enough to make sense when you read them later. Avoid using single words or phrases that are too short to be meaningful. Also, it is a good idea to list items as subtopics of a main idea, but do not try to follow a strict outline form. You do not want to waste time thinking, for example, "Is this letter *D* or number 5?" When you review your notes after class you can renumber or reletter the items if you want to clarify their relationship.

Take notes as you listen to the lecture "The End of the Universe" and then use your notes to complete the next exercise.

Understanding the Lecture. Test your comprehension of the lecture by circling the letter of the answer that best completes each of these statements. Use your notes to help you recall.

1. The world always needs more energy because when we use energy we _____ .
   a. destroy it
   (b.) change it to a less useful form

2. Energy always changes to a _____ .
   a. higher grade
   b. lower grade

3. All energy eventually winds up as _____ .
   a. muscle energy   b. heat energy

4. When you rub your hands, muscle energy changes to _____ .
   a. heat energy   b. kinetic energy

5. Energy always flows from _____ .
   a. hot to cold   b. cold to hot

6. Natural processes move from _____ .
   a. order to disorder   b. disorder to order

7. Perfume escaping into the air is an example of the change from _____ .
   a. order to disorder   b. potential energy to kinetic energy

8. Everything in the universe will eventually be in a state of _____ .
   a. order   b. disorder

Separate the salt and pepper?

9. We do not need to worry about the degeneration of the universe because it _____ .

   a. won't happen   b. won't happen for a long time

10. The main idea of this lecture is that energy _____ .
    a. can't be destroyed   b. runs downhill

DISCUSSION POINTS

Below are some nonscientific or "creative" definitions. They do not follow the formula for a scientific definition; instead, they are developed by the writer to express an opinion. For each of these creative definitions, tell what you think the writer meant and whether you agree with the writer.

1. Knowledge is the antidote to fear.—*Ralph Waldo Emerson*

2. Work consists of whatever a body is *obliged* to do, and play consists of whatever a body is not obliged to do.—*Mark Twain*

3. Genius is 1 percent inspiration, 99 percent perspiration.—*Thomas Alva Edison*

4. Art is I, Science is we.—*Claude Bernard*

5. Courage is resistance to fear, master of fear—not absence of fear.—*Mark Twain*

6. . . . Education means—to be able to do what you've never done before.—*George Herbert Palmer*

7. All life is an experiment. The more experiments you make the better.—*Ralph Waldo Emerson*

8. Knowledge is the knowing that we cannot know.—*Ralph Waldo Emerson*

WRITING SKILLS

Extended Definitions

A definition may consist of as little as a sentence or as much as a book. When a concept is too complex to be defined in one or two sentences, an extended definition is needed. An extended definition includes the basic parts of a formal definition (class + characteristics) as well as additional information that may include description, examples, classification, comparison, explanation, or other details. For example, an extended definition of a natural phenomenon (such as an eclipse, earthquake, or hurricane) would probably include causes and effects. An extended definition of a machine would probably include its functions and uses. An extended definition of a celestial object (such as a planet or comet) might include its location in respect to the earth and a comparison with another heavenly object. An extended definition of a disease would probably include its symptoms, prevention, and cure. An extended definition of an element or chemical would include where it occurs in nature and its chemical and physical properties.

Writing an Extended Definition

Write a paragraph giving an extended definition of a simple instrument or device such as a compass, fever thermometer, electric fan, pencil sharpener, flashlight, calculator, or toaster. Your topic sentence should be a formal definition, that is, the class plus distinguishing characteristics:

A thermometer is a device for measuring temperature.

A flashlight is a portable light that works on batteries.

The rest of the paragraph should include additional characteristics such as:

1. A description of its appearance, such as its shape, size and color;
2. A description of what it is made of; and
3. An explanation of its principle of operation or how it works.

A good way to conclude this type of definition is to describe its uses.

chapter 6

Exemplifying
Heat

INTRODUCTION

After giving a definition or making any general statement, the best way to clarify a point is to give an example of it. A Chinese proverb says that a picture is worth a thousand words. It might also be said that one example is worth a thousand explanations. An example brings the general or abstract statement down to a specific or concrete image. For example, it is one thing to say that smoking is bad for your health and another to say that a regular smoker loses about five and a half minutes of life expectancy for each cigarette smoked. The example adds impact, making the statement more memorable, more interesting, and more persuasive, as well as providing evidence for it.

Scientists use examples to explain or clarify a concept and to give evidence to support it. Examples can sometimes serve to test the validity of a point. If no example can be found to illustrate a point, there may not be a point.

Short Reading

Read the passage below and underline examples of how heat affects the properties of matter.

The Effects of Temperature

Temperature affects matter in many ways. As a substance gets hotter, its molecules move faster and its properties are altered. The physical state of a substance is affected by its temperature. For example, at a temperature of 0° C or below, water is a solid (ice); above 0° C it becomes a liquid; and at 100° C it turns to a gas (steam). Almost all other substances are similarly affected by temperature.

Temperature alters the color of matter. Iron, for example, turns red, then orange, and then white at increasingly high temperatures. (You have seen the iron burner on a stove turn red.) An incandescent light bulb provides another example of a color change, for its tungsten wire gives off a white light when it is hot.

The size of an object is affected by temperature. Most materials expand when they are heated and contract when they are cooled. A glass may break when boiling water is poured into it because part of the glass heats up and expands more rapidly than the rest.

Temperature also affects the pressure of a gas. As a gas is heated, its molecules begin to move rapidly, colliding with the walls of the container. If a closed glass tube is heated, the increased pressure inside will cause it to break.

The ability of a metal to resist electricity varies with its temperature. The increased movement of its molecules makes the molecules less resistant to electrical charge. Heated wires cause excess electrical movement, which can damage machines. Computers and other sensitive machines function best in air-conditioned rooms.

Living things are very sensitive to comparatively small temperature changes. This is exemplified when we touch something very hot or cold and feel pain. The pain serves to protect us, because living things cannot stand extremes of temperature. Using the same principle, we pasteurize milk and cook meat to kill harmful bacteria and other organisms that cannot tolerate the heat.

USING ENGLISH TO EXEMPLIFY

The above passage makes several claims about how temperature affects matter. Each statement is followed by specific examples that serve to illustrate the point.

The physical state of a substance is affected by its temperature.
(Examples make a point clearer and at the same time, give evidence to support it.)

For example, at a temperature of 0° C or below, water is a solid. . . .

Temperature alters the color of matter.
(An example may comprise a few words, a sentence, a paragraph or more.)

Iron, for example, turns red, then orange, and then white at increasingly higher temperatures.

The size of an object is affected by temperature.
(Examples are not always marked with clue words such as *for example, for instance,* and *to illustrate,* and often can only be identified by the context of the paragraph.)

A glass may break when boiling water is poured into it. . . .

Temperature also affects the pressure of a gas.

If a closed glass tube is heated, the increased pressure inside will cause it to break.

The ability of a metal to resist electricity varies with its temperature.

Heated wires cause excess electrical movement, which can damage machines.

Living things are very sensitive to comparatively small temperature changes.
(Sometimes more than one example is used to explain the various aspects of a concept.)

This is exemplified when we touch something very hot or cold and feel pain.

. . . We pasteurize milk and cook meat to kill harmful bacteria and other organisms that cannot tolerate heat.

Sentence Patterns

EXEMPLIFYING

For example,
For instance,
To be specific, } iron turns red when it is heated.
To illustrate,

Iron, {for example, / for instance,} turns red when heated.

Iron is {an example / a case / an instance / an illustration} of a substance that turns red when heated.

Iron {exemplifies / illustrates} the concept of heat affecting color.

The concept of heat affecting color is {exemplified / illustrated} by iron.

Solids {such as / like} iron and copper turn red when heated.

NOTE: When writing examples, remember the following:
1. *Examples in science are usually written in the present simple tense.*
2. *Examples are also used to illustrate terms, and these examples are similar to classification. For instance, the sentence,* Copper is an example of a metal, *is both an example and a classification. If all possible examples of a term are given, it is more classification than example.*
3. *Examples are* not *always marked with clue words and often can only be identified by the context of the paragraph.*

Analyzing Exemplification.   In each of these pairs or groups of sentences, underline the general statements once and the examples twice.

1. Carbohydrates are organic compounds. Organic compounds contain carbon in combination with hydrogen and oxygen.

2. Some birds travel enormous distances without resting. The ruddy turnstone flies nonstop from Alaska to Hawaii every year.

3. Parasites are living things that feed off other living things. The mistletoe plant lives off apple, maple, and poplar trees, causing them to die from malnutrition.

4. Several theories have been proposed to explain the nature of light. Christian Huygens suggested that light travels in waves. Albert Einstein proposed that light is transmitted as tiny particles, or photons.

5. Symbiosis is the coexistence of living things for their mutual benefit. Plant lice or aphids live with ants in a symbiotic relationship.

6. Atomic research has led to the development of artificially prepared elements. Einsteinium, fermium, californium, and berkelium are all manmade elements.

Recognizing Examples.   Each of these general statements is followed by three sentences. In each case, circle the letter(s) of the sentence(s) that best support the general statement. One, two, or three sentences may be circled.

1. There is little possibility that there is life on any other planet within our solar system.
   (a.) Mercury and Venus are too hot to support life.
   b. There are only nine planets in our solar system.
   (c.) Uranus, Neptune, and Pluto are extremely cold and dark.

2. Vitamins may be harmful in excessive doses.
   a. Vitamin C can be taken in large doses without harm.
   b. Excessive amounts of Vitamin A may increase susceptibility to disease.
   c. Vitamin D prevents the disease rickets.

3. Temperature may be measured by different types of thermometers.
   a. The Celsius and Fahrenheit thermometers measure relative temperature.
   b. A barometer measures atmospheric pressure.
   c. A Kelvin thermometer measures absolute temperature.

4. A machine is a device that transforms energy from one form to another.
   a. A car engine converts the chemical energy of gasoline into mechanical energy.
   b. The food we eat is converted into energy in our bodies.
   c. A generator or dynamo changes mechanical energy into electrical energy.

5. Energy has many forms.
   a. Nuclear energy comes from splitting the nucleus of uranium or plutonium atoms.
   b. Radiant energy comes in the form of sunlight, x-rays, or gamma rays.
   c. Energy may be converted from one form to another.

Modals of Necessity

In Chapter 4 you saw how modals are used to express probability. English modals are also used to express necessity. The modals of necessity are *must,** have to, should,* and *ought to.*

In scientific writing, these modals are used in special ways. *Should* and *must* appear most frequently, usually in the passive voice. *Must* expresses a very strong need. It implies that anything else is impossible.

A speed of 18,000 miles per hour *must be maintained* **for the satellite to remain in orbit.**

Should is more moderate than *must* and sometimes expresses a recommendation.

This crop *should be watered* **every day during the dry season.**

However, in technical instructions, particularly for warnings, *should* is frequently used to mean *must.*

All nonessential personnel *should be evacuated* **from the area of the explosion.**

All nonessential personnel *must be evacuated* **from the area of the explosion.**

These two sentences have the same meaning.

Using Modals of Necessity. To each of the following sentences, add *must* and use the passive form of the verb in parentheses.

1. X-rays _____*must only be administered*_____ (only administer) when necessary.

2. Hydrochloric acid _____ (prepare) by heating sodium chloride with concentrated sulfuric acid.

3. For the body to combat germs, white blood cells _____ (produce) in the body.

4. The generator _____ (always turn off) before an inspection.

5. The vapors of carbon tetrachloride are poisonous and _____ _____ (not inhale).

Must is also used to express strong probability. For example, *There must be a leak in this valve.*

6. For human life to begin, an egg cell in the female _____

_____ (fertilize) by a sperm.

7. Potassium _____ (never allow) to come

in contact with water.

8. The facepiece seal on an oxygen breathing apparatus _____

_____ (never release) in an unsafe atmosphere, even if

inhalation becomes difficult.

Formulating Sentences with Necessity. Formulate sentences using *should* in the passive voice, following the pattern of the first pair of sentences, below.

1. The electricity is not shut off.

   The electricity should be shut off.

2. The blood donors are not being tested for anemia.
3. The radiation monitoring devices are not being calibrated regularly.
4. A fire extinguisher is not available in the laboratory.
5. The explosive devices are not properly insulated.
6. The technicians are not being protected from excessive radiation.
7. The needles are not being sterilized before the injections.
8. The patients are not being immunized against the flu.

READING SKILLS

Vocabulary Building

Knowing whether a word is a noun, verb, adjective, or adverb will sometimes help you guess its meaning. For example, in the sentence, *The whale surfaced from time to time to breathe air*, you can figure out that the word *surfaced* is a verb in the past tense because it follows the subject (*whale*) and has an *-ed* ending. Then, the phrase *to breathe air* will give you the clue that *surfaced* means *came to the top*. In the sentence, *The moon revolves around the earth*, you could assume that *revolves* is an action, since it appears in the position of the verb. (The prepositional phrase *around the earth* gives you a further clue to its meaning.)

Suffixes are word endings like *-ed*, *-ly*, or *-ing*. They frequently offer clues to the word's part of speech. For example, you already know that the suffix *-ed* is used for verbs in the simple past tense and that the suffix *-ly* can be added to many adjectives (such as *soft* or *careful*) to make them adverbs (*softly*, *carefully*).

Suffixes: **-en, -ify, -cation**.   From the adjective *hard,* we can make the verb *to harden*, which means to make something hard. Convert each of these nouns and adjectives to verbs, using the suffix *-en*. If the word ends in *-e,* just add *-n.*

1. short *shorten* _____

2. broad _____

3. deep _____

4. dark _____

5. wide _____

6. weak _____

7. soft _____

8. black _____

9. tight _____

10. loose _____

11. bright _____

12. fright _____

13. strength _____

14. length _____

15. sharp _____

16. straight _____

Some verbs are formed with the suffix *-ify*. Write the appropriate form of the verb in the following spaces. The words with asterisks require some change in spelling. If necessary, check your dictionary.

1. to find the identity* *to identify* _____

2. to make solid _____

3. to make liquid* _____

4. to make pure* _____

5. to give an example* _____

6. to make humid _____

7. to charge with electricity* _____

8. to make clear* _____

The suffix *-cation* indicates a noun. Convert each of the *-ify* verbs above into a noun by changing the *y* to *i* and adding *-cation.*

1. *identification* _____

2. _____

3. _____

4. _____

5. _____

6. _____

7. _____

8. _____

Vocabulary in Context.   Circle the letter of the answer that best matches the meaning of the italicized word as it is used in each of these sentences.

1. To open the door, first *insert* the key in the lock.
   a. turn   (b.) enter

2. The submarine was completely *submerged* in the water and could not be seen.
   a. sunk   b. uncovered

3. Sound cannot be *conducted* in a vacuum because there are no air waves to transmit it.
   a. carried   b. absorbed

4. Wires were *insulated* to prevent the transfer of electricity or heat.
   a. covered   b. exposed

5. *Fluids* are not rigid and can flow from one container to another.
   a. solids   b. liquids and gases

6. Germs are *invisible* without the aid of a microscope.
   a. unable to be seen   b. unable to be divided

7. After the fire, the nuclear reactor was *emitting* radiation.
   a. giving off   b. absorbing

8. The sun *radiates* heat and light.
   a. takes in   b. gives off

9. When there is a *disparity* between test results, the test should be repeated.
   a. similarity   b. difference

Scanning

Scan the following passage in three minutes or less and put brackets around the following:

1. One example of conduction,
2. one example of convection, and
3. one example of radiation.

Keep in mind that examples usually come directly after definitions or general statements.

Reading

How Heat Is Transferred

Heat is the energy that warms our houses and cooks our food. It is the transfer of energy from a warmer body to a cooler body. How does this heat transfer take place?

Conduction is one method of heat transfer that takes place when there is a difference in temperature between two objects. For example, if a silver spoon is inserted into a pot of hot tea, the handle of the spoon will immediately become hot. This is because the molecules at the submerged end speed up, which causes the slow-moving molecules at the cold end to move faster. Energy is thus transferred or conducted.

Heat flows from a warmer object to a cooler one until the temperatures are equal. Substances like metals are good conductors because heat transfers readily from one molecule to another. All substances conduct some heat, but substances like glass, plastic, and wood act as insulators because their molecules transfer energy so slowly. Gases and liquids are poor conductors because the molecules make very little contact with which to pass on the energy. The warmest materials are those that trap pockets of air, such as wool, fiberglass, asbestos, and down. A vacuum would make an ideal insulator because it has no molecules to transfer the heat.

Although molecules in a fluid do not conduct heat very well, they do transfer heat by convection. Convection is the upward flow of masses of liquid or gas molecules as they are heated from below. The hot air rising above a radiator is an example of convection. As the heat causes the air to expand, it becomes less dense and rises. Convection is used in hot air furnaces, in which air is heated and then forced into a room to replace the cold air, which is then drawn into the furnace to be heated. Winds and ocean currents are examples of convection found in nature.

Radiation is the third method of heat transfer. All life on earth is dependent on the radiation of the sun's heat and light energy. One fascinating aspect of the sun's radiation is that the electromagnetic rays that carry warmth and light to the earth are themselves invisible and without heat. We know this because the space between the earth and the sun is dark and cold, but when the rays reach the earth, they light the atmosphere and warm our world. In contrast to conducted and convected heat, radiated heat passes through a vacuum.

All things give off radiation.

All objects emit, or give off, radiation. For example, when two objects are near each other, the one that is warmer will give off more energy than the cooler one, thus transferring energy from one to the other. Usually, objects do not absorb all the energy but reflect some of it. Light colors reflect more energy than dark colors. Highly polished surfaces reflect more energy than dull ones.

The three modes of heat transfer—conduction, convection, and radiation—are subject to two conditions: First, heat is transferred only when there is a disparity in temperature, and second, the flow is always from hot to cold.

Drawing Conclusions.   A scientist must be able to draw conclusions from the available facts. For example, if it is true that wood is a better insulator than metal, it is a logical conclusion that wood would make a better pot handle than metal.

After reading the previous passage carefully, indicate what conclusions can be drawn from the information it contains by circling the letter of the answer that best completes each of these sentences.

1. If the molecules in your tea are moving very rapidly, your tea is
   _____ .
   a. hot   b. cold

2. Opening the door between a warm room and a cold one will cause the
   temperature in the two rooms to _____ .
   a. equalize   b. increase

3. Oxygen is a _____ conductor of heat.
   a. good   b. poor

4. A double-glass window that traps air is a _____ insulator.
   a. good   b. poor

5. Since cork has air pockets, it is a _____ insulator.
   a. good   b. poor

6. An air conditioner that causes hot air to rise operates on the principle of
   _____ .
   a. conduction   b. convection

7. On a trip from the earth to the moon you would pass through _____
   temperatures.
   a. cold   b. hot

8. The earth absorbs heat _____ .
   a. and radiates it   b. but doesn't radiate it

9. The most comfortable clothing on a hot, sunny day is _____ .
   a. light colored   b. dark colored

10. A house with white walls will be _____ than one with dark walls.
   a. cooler   b. warmer

LISTENING SKILLS

Vocabulary in Context. Circle the letter of the answer that best matches the meaning of the italicized word as it is used in each of these sentences.

1. The *subtraction* of all the air created a vacuum.
   a. addition   (b.) removal

2. The *conversion* of a wormlike caterpillar into a beautiful butterfly is fascinating to watch.
   a. transformation   b. separation

3. The climate of the earth may be *gradually* becoming warmer.
   a. slowly   b. rapidly

4. There is *sufficient* gasoline in the car to make the trip but not to return.
   a. high quality   b. enough

5. A liquid will *solidify* if cooled enough.
   a. melt   b. harden

6. Perfume will *evaporate* quickly from an open bottle.
   a. vaporize   b. liquefy

7. The wind *dispersed* the leaves all over the field.
   a. gathered   b. scattered

8. Ammonia must be kept in a container with a tightly closed lid because it *is volatile*.
   a. evaporates   b. liquefies

9. A desert climate is characterized by a lack of *moisture* in the air.
   a. wetness   b. dryness

10. The world population is increasing at an alarming *rate*.
    a. place   b. speed

11. When opposite chemical reactions occur at the same rate, a state of *equilibrium* exists.
    a. disorder   b. balance

12. The ratio of hydrogen to oxygen in water is *constant*.
    a. changing   b. unchanging

Note-Taking

When taking notes during a lecture, concentrate on the main ideas. However, if you have time, also write down additional details such as examples. As in written material, examples in a lecture usually come directly after the points they illustrate. Examples will help you understand and remember any point that is difficult or unfamiliar. They can also be used to prove or substantiate your point when writing an answer to an essay question.

Take notes as you listen to the lecture "The Changing State of Matter" and then use your notes to complete the next exercise.

Understanding the Lecture.   Indicate whether each of the following statements is true (*T*) or false (*F*) according to the information in the lecture.

_____*T*_____ 1. A change of state cannot occur without adding or subtracting heat.

_____ 2. Only a few substances can convert from one physical state to another.

_____ 3. The conversion of a solid to a liquid is called evaporation.

_____ 4. All substances melt at the same temperature.

_____ 5. Gases such as oxygen cannot be solidified.

_____ 6. Heating a liquid causes the molecules to move faster.

_____ 7. Fog is an example of evaporation.

_____ 8. A volatile substance is one that is stable.

_____ 9. Alcohol is a volatile liquid.

_____ 10. The condensation point is the same as the boiling point.

_____ 11. Equilibrium exists when the rate of condensation and the rate of evaporation are the same.

_____ 12. Clouds are formed by the process of evaporation.

DISCUSSION POINTS

Give one or two examples of each of the following. Explain your answers.

1. Scientific facts that still amaze you.
2. Machines you would not want to live without.
3. Machines you wish had never been invented.
4. Scientific discoveries you would like to have witnessed.
5. Things you would like someone to invent.
6. Places you would like to explore.
7. Things you think scientists will never know.

WRITING SKILLS

Exemplifying

Exemplifying is one of the most useful ways of explaining or clarifying a point. Broad, general statements are frequently neither interesting nor persuasive. Examples help the reader move from the abstract to the concrete level and thus visualize the writer's point. In scientific writing in particular examples help establish the credibility of a statement. If you are making an argument, examples will help convince your readers. Finally, examples are the element of your writing most likely to remain in your reader's mind. Consider the following:

Almost all embryonic animals have extensive regenerative capacities. Some animals retain these capacities after they reach maturity, while others lose them. An adult sea star or hydra can be chopped into many pieces and each piece can regenerate all necessary parts to become a whole individual. Half a planarian can regenerate the other half. Salamanders and lizards can regenerate new tails. But adult birds and mammals cannot regenerate whole new organs; regeneration in these animals is mostly limited to the healing of wounds.

William T. Keeton,
Elements of Biological Science
(New York: W. W. Norton & Co., 1973), p. 349

Notice how the examples make the topic sentence clear and memorable. In fact, the examples enable readers to understand the topic sentence even if they do not know the meaning of *regenerative capacity* or *embryonic animals*.

Writing a Paragraph with Examples

Write a paragraph on one of the Discussion Points. Begin with a topic sentence and then support it with examples. Transition words for introducing examples include *for example, for instance, to illustrate, such as*, and *like*. Be sure to give an example to illustrate every aspect of your idea. For example, if you state that there are things we will never know about the universe, humans beings, the past, and the future, give examples of some of these things we will never know. If you give several examples to support one idea, arrange them in order of increasing importance. This will make your writing more forceful because your strongest example will be in the part of the paragraph that has the most emphasis or impact.

chapter 7

Giving Evidence

Smoking, Drugs, and Alcohol

INTRODUCTION

Once a hypothesis has been proposed, the question is always asked, "Where is the evidence?" The British scientist Sir Humphry Davy once burned diamonds into graphite, ignoring the expense, to demonstrate that diamonds and graphite are both crystallized carbon. He made his point.

Proof or evidence is usually the result of observation or experimentation, combined with reasoning. The theories that are accepted are those with the most supporting evidence. In the second century, Claudius Ptolemy proposed that the planets and the sun revolved around the earth. His theory was accepted because it predicted the position of the planets with some accuracy. But all "proofs" are tentative, to be discarded when another theory emerges that explains more facts. Thirteen centuries later, the Polish scientist Nicolaus Copernicus "proved" that the planets revolve around the sun by demonstrating that his theory explained things that Ptolemy's theory could not, like the seasons of the earth and the retrograde or backward motion of the planets. Then, in 1905 Albert Einstein shook everyone up by saying that motion is relative and that whether the sun is moving or the earth is moving depends on your point of view! And on and on we go, always striving to get closer and closer to the truth. But scientific theories can seldom be proven beyond a doubt. After all, no one can stand far enough out in space to observe the planets revolving around the sun!

Short Reading

Read the following passage to discover evidence that smoking is harmful.

Where There's Smoke, There's Fire

It was not too long ago that smoking by adults was not viewed as dangerous. Its long-term effects were not visible and had not been conclusively demonstrated. Then, in 1964 the Surgeon General of the United States announced that smoking had been proven by scientific research to be detrimental, or harmful, to health.

Since then, more and more evidence has accumulated to indicate that smoking is harmful. Smoking is related to many heart and circulatory ailments. The tobacco plant contains nicotine, a chemical that is poison in its pure form. It has been demonstrated that nicotine increases the rate of the heart, intensifies the effects of high blood pressure, and causes the constriction or tightening of the blood vessels, thus contributing to heart disease.

Smoking is the most significant factor in respiratory diseases. It can damage the tiny hairs (cilia) that line the breathing passages, thereby causing emphysema or chronic bronchitis. Research also confirms that the tar in cigarette smoke is carcinogenic, that is, it can produce cancer in any tissues it comes in contact with, such as the mouth, the throat, and the lungs.

There is also a correlation between smoking and birth defects. The evidence indicates that pregnant women who smoke a pack of cigarettes a day have a greater likelihood of having a miscarriage, a premature baby, a smaller-than-normal baby, or a baby with mental retardation or heart defects.

Smokers often become physically and psychologically dependent on their habit and suffer withdrawal symptoms if they attempt to stop. Even the onset of a smoking-related illness is not always sufficient to enable heavy smokers to quit. Despite all the information made available to the public since 1964, in 1985 the American Lung Association estimated that there were 250,000 premature deaths due to smoking in the United States per year.

USING ENGLISH TO GIVE EVIDENCE

The main point, or hypothesis, of the previous passage is that smoking is dangerous to your health. The argument is based on four statements, each of which is supported by evidence. (Note that scientific evidence must be fact, *not* opinion.)

Smoking is related to many heart and circulatory ailments.
(Evidence is frequently introduced with words like *indicates* or *demonstrates* rather than the stronger word *proves*. This reflects the "unprovable" nature of most scientific hypotheses.)

It has been demonstrated that nicotine increases the rate of the heart. . . .

Smoking is the most significant factor in respiratory diseases.

It can damage the tiny hairs (cilia) that line the breathing passages. . . .

Research also confirms that the tar in cigarette smoke is carcinogenic. . . .

There is also a correlation between smoking and birth defects.

The evidence indicates that pregnant women who smoke a pack of cigarettes a day have a greater likelihood of having a miscarriage. . . .

Smokers often become physically and psychologically dependent on their habit. . . .
(Evidence is not always marked with a clue word and often can only be identified by the context of the paragraph.)

Smokers often . . . suffer withdrawal symptoms if they attempt to stop.

Even the onset of a smoking-related illness is not always sufficient to enable heavy smokers to quit.

Identifying Evidence.   In each of these pairs of statements, underline the conclusion once and the evidence twice.

1. <u>A plastic raincoat prevents the rain from penetrating, but a wool coat does not</u>. <u><u>Plastic is impermeable to water, and wool is not</u></u>.

2. If a bottle of perfume is left open in a closed room, the smell will eventually spread all over the room. The molecules of a gas spread, or diffuse, to fill the entire area.

3. The earth is round. A person traveling directly east from the equator will eventually return to the starting place.

4. A bell rung in a vacuum makes no sound. Sound is only produced when there are molecules to transmit it.

5. Life as we know it cannot exist on Venus. There is no oxygen or water on Venus.

6. Morphine is addictive. Hospital patients who are given morphine as a pain reliever sometimes develop a physical dependence on the drug.

7. Death often occurs when drugs and alcohol are used together. Certain combinations of alcohol and drugs can be fatal.

8. Glass is fragile, or breakable. A glass bottle dropped on a hard surface is likely to break.

Drawing Conclusions from Evidence.   Circle the letter of the conclusion that can be drawn from each of these statements of evidence.

1. When the water in a closed bottle is heated, the water rises.
   a. Water evaporates when heated.
   b. Water expands when heated.

2. The shapes of the earth's continents fit together like pieces of a big jigsaw puzzle.
   a. The continents were once one land mass that broke into parts that drifted apart.
   b. The earth is expanding just as the universe is.

3. There is a high statistical correlation between smoking and emphysema.
   a. Emphysema patients like to smoke.
   b. Smoking is a cause of emphysema.

4. The space between the sun and the earth is cold.
   a. The sun is not as hot as it used to be.
   b. The rays of the sun warm what they touch but are not hot themselves.

5. In a crowded room, carbon dioxide gradually replaces the oxygen in the air.
   a. Human beings inhale oxygen and exhale carbon dioxide.
   b. Human beings inhale carbon dioxide and exhale oxygen.

6. When a bean seed is grown in the dark, the plant soon dies.
   a. Bean plants need light to survive.
   b. Bean plants need light to turn green.

7. Alcohol can blur your vision.
   a. Alcohol affects driving ability.
   b. Alcohol does not affect driving ability.

Evaluating Evidence.   After each of the following propositions, several statements are given. Circle the letters of those statements that give evidence or support for the proposition. There may be more than one answer for each.

1. Alcohol is dangerous for drivers.
   a. Alcohol is addictive.
   b. Alcoholics build up a tolerance for increasing amounts of alcohol.
   c. Alcohol impairs judgment.
   d. Many automobile accidents are alcohol related.

2. Aluminum is a light metal.
   a. Aluminum is produced from bauxite.
   b. Aluminum is one of the most abundant elements.
   c. Aluminum weighs less than iron, zinc, silver, gold, and copper.
   d. The melting point of aluminum is 660° C.

3. Water expands when it freezes.
   a. Water pipes sometimes crack in very cold weather.
   b. Water freezes at 0° C.
   c. Different substances freeze at different temperatures.
   d. Most substances contract when frozen.

4. Oxygen supports combustion.
   a. Blowing on a fire makes it burn more brightly.
   b. Forest fires are worse in a strong wind.
   c. Nitrogen does not support combustion.
   d. Smothering a fire will put it out.

5. Vitamin A is essential for a healthy diet.
   a. Lack of vitamin A may cause night blindness.
   b. Vitamin A is found in butter, eggs, and fish liver oils.
   c. Vitamin A aids the cells in fighting infection.
   d. An overdose of vitamin A can be toxic.

6. When water vapor comes in contact with a cold surface, it condenses or forms droplets of water.
   a. Eyeglasses cloud up when you enter a warm room from the cold.
   b. Raindrops formulate when clouds meet cold air.
   c. Dew forms on grass overnight.
   d. Rain turns to snow when the temperature drops below 0° C.

Deductive and Inductive Reasoning

Scientists use two basic methods to move from evidence to a conclusion: deductive reasoning and inductive reasoning. Deductive reasoning moves from a general premise or assumption to a specific conclusion. For example:

All metals are good conductors of electricity.
Zinc is a metal.
Therefore, zinc is a good conductor of electricity.

In contrast, inductive reasoning moves from a specific observation to a general conclusion. For example, if air is observed to expand or contract to fill any container, the assumption might be made that all gases behave this way. As a matter of fact, they do.

Deductive reasoning is always valid, that is, if it is properly stated and if the premises are true, the conclusion will be true. The conclusion is contained in the premises. By contrast, inductive reasoning can lead to false conclusions. For example, we might assume that if a particular mushroom is poisonous, all mushrooms must be poisonous. That would be a false assumption. Nevertheless, inductive reasoning can be very valuable in alerting the scientist to potential principles that must then be tested before they can be accepted.

Identifying Deductive and Inductive Reasoning.   Indicate whether each of the following statements illustrates deductive (*D*) or inductive (*I*) reasoning.

_____*I*_____ 1. Iron silicates are green, iron carbonates are yellow-brown, and iron oxides are red. All iron compounds are colorful.

_____ 2. Smoke causes cancer in rats. Smoke causes cancer in all living things.

_____ 3. Tigers, horses, and dogs have tails. All four-legged animals have tails.

_____ 4. Carbohydrates convert starch into sugar in the body. Potatoes are carbohydrates. Potatoes convert starch into sugar.

_____ 5. Penicillin stops the growth of bacteria. Pneumonia is caused by bacteria. Penicillin is effective against pneumonia.

_____ 6. AIDS is a venereal disease. It is sometimes transmitted by blood. All venereal diseases may be transmitted by blood.

_____ 7. Halley's Comet passed near the earth in 1758, 1834, 1910, and 1986. Halley's Comet will return to the earth in the year 2062.

_____ 8. Automobiles give off carbon monoxide. Carbon monoxide is a poisonous gas. Therefore automobiles cause air pollution.

Using Reasoning.   Deductive reasoning can sometimes lead to false conclusions. Here are two examples:

All students are lazy.
Everyone here is a student.
Therefore, everyone here is lazy.

All gases can flow.
All liquids can flow.
Therefore, all gases are liquids.

How did we arrive at such ridiculous conclusions? In the first example the original premise is false. False premises lead to false conclusions. In the second example, the conclusion does not follow from the premises, for although gases and liquids share one characteristic (both can flow), this does not mean they are the same in other ways.

Inductive reasoning can also lead to false conclusions. Sometimes there are not enough examples. Sometimes the examples are not representative or not typical. And sometimes the conclusion does not follow from the evidence.

In each of the following, discuss why the conclusion is false.

1. If it is a bird, it can fly.
   A chicken cannot fly.
   Therefore, a chicken is not a bird.
2. Einstein was not a good student.
   Einstein was a genius.
   Therefore, anyone who is not a good student is a genius.
3. All metals are solid.
   Sulfur is a solid.
   Therefore, sulfur is a metal.
4. People, kangaroos, penguins, and ostriches all walk on two feet.
   Therefore, they are members of the same species.
5. Archimedes discovered the principle of water displacement in the bathtub.
   The displacement principle is a major scientific discovery.
   Therefore, the place to make a major scientific discovery is in the bathtub.
6. Some elements are gases, and others are liquids.
   Sulfur is an element, and it is not a gas.
   Therefore, sulfur is a liquid.

7. Oak wood is lighter than water.
   Therefore, solids are lighter than liquids.
8. Either Galileo was a genius or he worked hard.
   Galileo was a genius.
   Therefore, Galileo did not work hard.
9. Marijuana has not been proven to be harmful.
   Therefore, marijuana is not a dangerous drug.
10. If it is an animal, it has a tail.
    A comet has a tail.
    Therefore, a comet is an animal.

READING SKILLS

Vocabulary Building

A synonym is a word that means the same as another word. Replace each italicized word in the following paragraph with a synonym from the list below. You will not use all the words listed.

insufficient	tolerance	stimulates
convince	irritability	deter
doses	detrimental	fatigued
calms	alert	beneficial

According to legend, coffee was discovered by a monk in the Middle Ages who noticed how frisky his goats were after they had eaten berries from a coffee tree. Coffee contains caffeine, a substance that *excites* the nervous system. Moderate *portions* of caffeine make the user feel less *tired* and more *awake*. High doses can be *harmful*, causing *excitability*. It is possible to increase *endurance* for caffeine so that higher doses are needed to produce the same effect. In certain places of the Middle East, there were times when coffee drinking was punishable by death, which probably was *not enough* to *persuade* some people to give up their morning cup.

Suffixes: -ion, -or.   Change the following verbs to nouns by adding the suffix *-ion*. Drop the final *-e* if it exists. Words with an asterisk require a spelling change. Check your dictionary if necessary.

1. to connect *connection* _____

2. to conduct _____

3. to radiate _____

4. to insulate _____

5. to accelerate _____

6. to gravitate _____

7. to lubricate _____

8. to calculate _____

9. to eliminate _____

10. to attract _____

11. to absorb* _____

12. to correlate _____

13. to exert _____

14. to speculate _____

15. to extend* _____

16. to demonstrate _____

17. to formulate _____

Change the following verbs to nouns by adding the suffix -*or*. Drop the final -*e* if it exists.

1. to connect *connector* _____

2. to radiate _____

3. to insulate _____

4. to resist _____

5. to accelerate _____

6. to demonstrate _____

7. to correlate _____

8. to speculate _____

9. to lubricate _____

10. to calculate _____

Vocabulary in Context.   Circle the letter of the answer that best matches the meaning of the italicized word as it is used in each of these sentences.

1. The drought *altered* conditions for the farmers.
   a. improved   b. changed

2. Cigarette smoking is so *addictive,* that many people cannot give it up.
   a. habit forming   b. unhealthy

3. She was lonely and suffered from *depression.*
   a. sadness   b. disease

4. Aspirin will frequently *relieve* pain for a few hours.
   a. ease   b. worsen

5. Poor physical condition will make you more *susceptible* to illness.
   a. sensitive   b. resistant

6. Virus *infections* cannot be cured with antibiotics.
   a. diseases   b. organisms

7. The accident victim did not know what happened because he was *in a coma.*
   a. unconscious   b. awake

8. Calcium is *obtained* from the electrolysis of calcium chloride.
   a. destroyed   b. gotten

9. Coffee *stimulates* the nerve centers.
   a. quiets   b. excites

10. The view from the mountain produced a *sensation* of dizziness.
    a. fear   b. feeling

11. He retired from his job when he developed a *chronic* illness.
    a. long lasting   b. brief

12. The needle was sterilized before the *injection.*
    a. insertion   b. removal

13. The *initial* research was inconclusive, so a second experiment was planned.
    a. last   b. first

14. The mountain climbers suffered from *exhaustion* when they reached the top.
    a. fatigue   b. hunger

15. AIDS is a *fatal* illness for everyone who contracts it.
    a. deadly   b. mild

16. To lose weight, he took pills to *suppress* his appetite.
    a. release   b. restrain

17. A straight stick submerged in water will appear *distorted.*
    a. out of shape   b. colored

18. Human beings have little *tolerance for* extremes in temperature.
    a. fear of   b. resistance to

19. The experiment had *consequences* that were not anticipated.
    a. causes   b. results

Skimming

Skimming for main ideas is a reading skill that is useful in a number of ways:

1. Always skim a textbook chapter before reading it closely. If you follow this procedure, you will read faster and with greater interest and comprehension.
2. When you need to write a research paper, skim the references you find in the library to see which contain the material you need.
3. Skim any passage that you find difficult. Once you have a general idea of the content and organization, you will be able to read it thoroughly with better understanding.

See p. 27 to review skimming techniques.
Skim the following passage in three minutes and then answer these questions:

1. Which of the following is the main idea?
    a. Drugs are always potentially harmful.
    b. Drugs are not harmful.
    c. Drugs are occasionally harmful but usually beneficial.
2. Which of the following drugs are discussed in the passage:
    cocaine, amphetamines, PCP, inhalants, narcotics, caffeine, marijuana, barbiturates, and hashish?

Reading

The Danger of Drugs

Drugs are substances that alter the body chemistry. The pleasing effects of any drug should be weighed carefully against its serious dangers.

Marijuana is a drug that has been much discussed and debated. It relaxes the mind and body and produces a pleasant, happy feeling in many users. At the same time, it can alter functions that may affect the memory, coordination, motivation, and attention span of the user. Although its effects may be less harmful than alcohol, it should not be assumed that it, or any drug, is harmless.

Narcotics (codeine, heroin, opium and morphine) are considered "hard drugs" and are addictive, or habit forming. They act as depressants on the nervous system, relieving pain and decreasing alertness and vigor. Heroin makes the user lethargic and highly susceptible to infection, coma, and even death from overdose. Because heroin is addictive, it often leads the user to crime to pay for the high cost of obtaining the drug. Another narcotic, morphine, is used by hospitals as a pain reliever. Occasionally, patients receiving morphine become addicted.

Cocaine (or "coke") is a drug that stimulates the nervous system, producing a feeling of well-being and strong sensations. Sniffing cocaine powder over a long period can cause paranoia, hyperactivity, and chronic insomnia. "Crack," a form of cocaine that is smoked, is especially dangerous because the user can become intensely addicted in a very short period of time. Like heroin, it frequently leads the user to crime.

Amphetamines (called "speed" or "uppers") include Benzedrine, Dexedrine, and Methedrine. These drugs increase the blood pressure and stimulate the nervous system to give the user great bursts of energy. In small amounts, they are used by students and drivers to stay awake, by athletes to improve their physical performance, and by dieters to decrease their appetite. However, injections of amphetamines bring on initial feelings of energy and well-being that are followed by low periods of depression, exhaustion, irritability, and aggressiveness. An overdose of amphetamines can be fatal.

Barbiturates, or "downers" (sleeping pills), act on areas of the brain to reduce anxiety and cause sleepiness. The effects include loss of muscle coordination, slurred speech, and mental confusion. The use of barbiturates and alcohol together can suppress the breathing centers and be fatal.

Psychedelics, or hallucinogens (including LSD and mescaline), are drugs that produce hallucinations and other mental disorders. Their effects are somewhat unpredictable. Psychedelics can cause changes in mood, thinking, and behavior and distortions of time and space. Effects include dizziness, nausea, anxiety, and tremors.

With the exception of marijuana, research indicates that most of the above drugs are addictive. Users build up a tolerance for the drug, requiring increasing doses to achieve the same effects. Sometimes an addict's tolerance may be dangerously high, and a fatal amount is taken accidentally. Anyone considering using any drug should be aware of the potentially serious consequences.

Understanding the Reading.   Indicate whether each of the following statements is true (*T*) or false (*F*) according to the previous passage.

_____*F*_____ 1. Only certain drugs alter the body's chemistry.

_____ 2. There is no correlation between the use of marijuana and a decrease in motivation.

_____ 3. Marijuana is less dangerous than alcohol and therefore is probably harmless.

_____ 4. Morphine cannot become addictive when used by hospitals as a pain reliever.

_____ 5. A significant danger of heroin is that it is so addictive.

_____ 6. Cocaine has no long-term harmful effects.

_____ 7. Cocaine is one drug that is not addictive.

_____ 8. Some students use amphetamines because they provide temporary bursts of energy.

_____ 9. Even an overdose of amphetamines will probably not be fatal.

_____ 10. Barbiturates are particularly dangerous when taken with alcohol.

_____ 11. Scientists can predict with reasonable accuracy the effects of LSD on the user.

_____ 12. A user who builds up a tolerance for a drug is in danger of a fatal overdose.

LISTENING SKILLS

Vocabulary in Context. Circle the letter of the answer that best matches the meaning of the italicized word as it is used in each of these sentences.

1. Cocaine has *physiological* as well as psychological effects.
   a. physical   b. mental

2. Exercise is *beneficial* for a healthy individual.
   a. dangerous   b. good

3. The message was *transmitted* by electronic mail.
   a. received   b. sent

4. The accident occurred because the driver was *intoxicated*.
   a. arrested   b. drunk

5. Old age brings the gradual *degeneration* of the body.
   a. strengthening   b. weakening

6. High doses of radiation can affect reproduction and cause a person to be *sterile*.
   a. strong   b. unable to have children

7. Sugar has a *detrimental* effect on your teeth.
   a. harmless   b. harmful

8. Dust *accumulated* on the engine, impairing its function.
   a. evaporated   b. gathered

9. If a tail is cut off, a lizard has the *capacity* to grow a new one; a cat does not.
   a. need   b. ability

10. The condition of the building *deteriorated* because the tenants did not take proper care of it.
    a. worsened   b. improved

Note-Taking

After writing down main ideas, try to write down any evidence that supports these ideas. Facts, statistics, results of experiments, and explanations are worthwhile jotting down if you have time. The evidence reinforces the main concepts and helps you to recall them later.

Take notes as you listen to the lecture "The Physiological Effects of Alcohol." Try to write down evidence in addition to the main points. Then use your notes to complete the next exercise.

Understanding the Lecture.   Use your notes to determine whether each of the following statements is true (*T*) or false (*F*) according to the information in the lecture.

_____F_____ 1. Since small amounts of alcohol make people feel good, large amounts make them feel better.

_____ 2. Even small quantities of alcohol depress the heart rate.

_____ 3. Small quantities of alcohol may relieve tension.

_____ 4. The unclear speech and blurred vision of intoxicated people is evidence that alcohol affects the nervous system.

_____ 5. Alcoholism can inflame the muscles and cause enlargement of the heart.

_____ 6. Chronic alcoholism can cause sterility.

_____ 7. Although harmful in other ways, alcohol has a beneficial effect on the liver.

_____ 8. There is no evidence that alcohol affects the brain.

_____ 9. It is all right for pregnant women to consume alcohol after the early months of pregnancy.

_____ 10. Some people become addicted more easily than others.

_____ 11. Drinking strong black coffee will help a person overcome the effects of alcohol.

_____ 12. Short-term beneficial effects of alcohol are usually outweighed by long-term negative effects.

DISCUSSION POINTS

Be prepared to give your opinion on one of these topics, offering evidence for why you think the way you do.

1. Should advertising for cigarettes be banned?
2. Should advertising for alcohol be banned?
3. Should students be expelled from high school for using drugs on campus?
4. Should people convicted of drunken driving have their licenses taken away?
5. Should marijuana be legalized?
6. Should the minimum age for drinking be changed?
7. Should smoking be banned from public places?

WRITING SKILLS

Giving Evidence

Scientific writing requires that you provide evidence to support your statements. The more evidence you have and the better it is, the stronger your statement or argument will be. In Chapter 6 we discussed the use of examples, but there are other forms of evidence, including facts, statistics, observations, test results, survey results, and expert opinion. Discuss which of these forms of evidence are used in each of the examples below. (An example may include more than one form of evidence.)

1. The process of evolution may be over for human beings. For thousands of years, human beings have been changing their environment instead of being changed by it.
2. A danger exists that the ozone in the upper atmosphere may be destroyed by man-made chemicals, allowing harmful ultraviolet light to reach the earth. This was first discovered in 1983 by a team of British scientists who demonstrated that concentrations of ozone were decreasing in the stratosphere over Antarctica.
3. The death rate from traffic accidents on U.S. roads does not increase on holiday weekends. Although the number of fatalities increases by about one percent, there are about three percent more drivers on the roads.
4. Drinking appears to increase the incidence of hypertension, according to tests performed on adult men by researchers at Stanford University.
5. By the middle of the 21st century, a significant part of the world's electricity will be supplied by controlled thermonuclear fusion, according to reports issued by the U.S. Department of Energy.
6. Researchers at a midwestern college of medicine interviewed thirty creative writers and found an association between creativity and mental disorders such as depression and manic depression.

Writing with Evidence

Write a paragraph on one of the Discussion Points. First state your opinion as the topic sentence and then provide evidence to establish the credibility of your point. Conclude by summarizing your ideas, stating their significance, or recommending actions the reader might take.

chapter 8

Experimenting

Electricity and Magnetism

INTRODUCTION

The ancient Greek philosophers obtained their knowledge about the universe from reasoning and logic. But Galileo's experiments proved that Aristotle's reasoning was not always valid. Since then, no scientific concept is accepted unless there is evidence to support it.

When testing a hypothesis, every effort is made to eliminate subjective or biased ideas. If experiments do not support a hypothesis, the hypothesis must be rejected or modified. The twentieth-century writer-scientist Isaac Asimov wrote: "Even though billions of observers tend to bear out a generalization, a single observation that contradicts or is inconsistent with it must force its modification."*

Sometimes an experiment proves something other than what the researcher intended. Many great discoveries were accidents of an experiment. In 1929, for example, the Scottish researcher Sir Alexander Fleming noticed that some bacteria had been destroyed by a mold. He had accidentally discovered penicillin. In 1895, the German scientist Wilhelm Roentgen noticed that cathode rays penetrated black paper. Thus, x-rays were discovered. While experimenting, the scientist needs to keep a sharp eye and an open mind.

*Isaac Asimov, *Asimov's Guide to Science* (New York: Basic Books, 1972), p. 13.

Short Reading

Read the following passage to find directions for performing an experiment.

Lightning Strikes

You know that lightning is actually electricity. But how does lightning occur?

The ancient Greeks noticed that when they rubbed a piece of amber* with wool or fur, the amber would attract or pick up small pieces of leaves or dust. This was called the amber effect. The English word *electricity* comes from the Greek word *electron*, which means amber. To demonstrate this concept, perform the following experiment:

1. Arrange tiny pieces of paper on a table.
2. Rub a plastic comb with some woolen fabric.
3. Hold the comb over the pieces of paper and observe what happens. The paper should be attracted to the comb. (*Note*: The comb must be rubbed again to sustain its magnetic capacity.)

In the eighteenth century, scientists discovered that there are two types of electric charge. The American Benjamin Franklin named these charges positive and negative. It was noted that like charges repel each other and unlike charges attract each other.

In the experiment above, the magnetic effect occurs because rubbing the comb causes some electrons from the cloth to run on to the comb. The cloth then has fewer electrons (which are negative) and thus becomes positively charged. The comb therefore has additional electrons, giving it a negative charge. The comb attracts the paper because opposite charges attract. Similarly, you have probably experienced an electric shock when you removed synthetic clothing from a clothes dryer, combed your hair, or touched a metal doorknob after walking across a thick rug.

A spectacular example of this phenomenon occurs during a storm. Inside a cloud, currents of air rub against the raindrops. As the electrons are rubbed off, one cloud becomes positively charged and another negatively charged. The opposite charges attract each other, and an enormous spark of electricity jumps from one cloud to another or from a cloud to the ground. Thus, lightning is produced.

USING ENGLISH TO GIVE DIRECTIONS

An experiment is a kind of process. We analyze a substance, such as air, by separating and identifying its components. We analyze a process by breaking it down into steps or procedures and arranging them in chronological order (the order in which things happen).

*Amber is a hard, yellowish-brown substance found in certain soils.

Giving Directions to Perform a Process

It is usually preferable to write directions as a list of steps rather than a paragraph. The imperative form of the verb is used. The subject (you) is implied, never stated:

   1. *Arrange* **tiny pieces of paper on a table.**
   2. *Rub* **a plastic comb with some woolen fabric.**
   3. *Hold* **the comb over the pieces of paper and** *observe* **what happens. The paper should be attracted to the comb.**

Notice that a verb may give directions for both mental and physical activities. Notice also the parallel form of the above list. Every clause begins with an imperative verb. One sentence (*The paper should be . . .*) does not have an imperative verb because it does not give a direction.

Imperative Verbs

Imperative verbs:

1. give a command or direction;
2. appear at the beginning of a clause;
3. have a subject that is implied, *not* stated (you); and
4. are formed from the present tense of the verb.

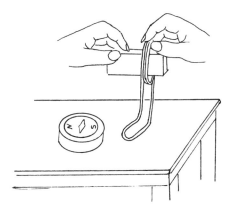

Recognizing Imperative Verbs.   Below are the directions for performing an experiment showing how magnetism produces electricity. Notice that each item is a separate step in the process. Underline all the imperative verbs.

1. <u>Make</u> several loops in a coil of wire.

2. Tie the ends of the wire together.

3. Insert a magnet through the coil.

4. Move the magnet back and forth through the coil.

5. Place a compass near the wire but away from the magnet.

6. Check the compass to see if the needle is moving. (A moving needle indicates that electric current is flowing through the wire and that magnetism can produce electricity.)

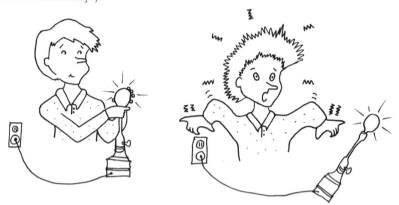

Remove the bulb . . . after disconnecting the electricity.

Arranging Items Chronologically.   When explaining a process, it is essential to describe steps in the order in which they happen, that is chronologically. Number each group of steps below in chronological order. The first step has been indicated in each list.

1. The heart pumps blood through the human body.

    __3__ The oxygen-rich blood returns to the left side of the heart.

    __1__ The right side of the heart pumps blood into the lungs.

    __4__ From the left side of the heart, the blood is pumped out to the rest of the body through the arteries and returns to the heart through the veins.

    __2__ In the lungs, the blood gives up carbon dioxide (which we breathe out) and absorbs oxygen.

2. It is easy to print a simple message on this computer.

    _____ Turn off the computer.

    _____ Type the first line.

    __1__ Turn on the computer.

    _____ Press the RETURN key after typing each line.

    _____ Press the PRINT key before typing each line.

3. The age of a rock is calculated by measuring the amount of its uranium that has been converted to lead.

_____*1*_____ Uranium, a radioactive element, changes into thorium.

_____ Lead is not radioactive and remains stable.

_____ Radium converts to lead.

_____ Thorium, also radioactive, turns to radium.

4. Mitosis is the process of cell division.

_____*1*_____ When a cell grows to a certain size, it begins to divide.

_____ A cell wall forms through the center of the cell.

_____ Two separate "daughter cells" have thus been completely formed.

_____ The cell's chromosomes begin to separate into two groups and pull toward opposite ends of the cell.

5. The power of a nuclear explosion is produced by the splitting of the atom.

_____ This results in a chain reaction of splitting atoms, releasing an enormous amount of energy.

_____ The other neutrons then split other uranium atoms.

_____*1*_____ When the nucleus of a uranium atom is hit by a neutron, the nucleus splits, giving off other neutrons.

6. Soil formation is a long process.

_____ Good soil has been formed.

_____ Then plants die and decompose, thus adding humus to the tiny pieces of rock.

_____*1*_____ First wind, sand, and rain wear away the rocks, producing tiny particles.

_____ Earthworms and insects overturn the rocks and humus, mixing everything up.

Using Imperative Verbs.   Using the following illustration as a guide, write directions for making an electromagnet with a battery, insulated wire, and a nail. Begin each step with an imperative verb and make sure all steps are in chronological order.

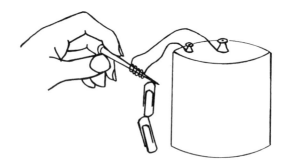

Verb Forms: Infinitives and Gerunds

In an English sentence, when one verb follows another, the second verb can take one of three forms:

1. an infinitive (*to advance, to detect*),
2. an infinitive without *to* (*advance, detect*), or
3. a gerund (*advancing, detecting*).

Students of English as a second language frequently find this confusing. How do you determine which form of the verb to use? The answer is that the first verb determines the form of the second. For example, the verb *begin* may be followed by an infinitive or a gerund. The verb *plan* must be followed by an infinitive. The modal *must* may only be followed by an infinitive without *to*. The verb *observe* may be followed by a gerund or an infinitive without *to*. Here are some examples:

> **Einstein *began to study* the photoelectric effect.**
> **Einstein *began studying* the photoelectric effect.**
> **Researchers *planned to repeat* the experiment.**
> **Researchers *must repeat* the experiment.**
> **Astronomers *observed* the supernova *exploding*.**
> **Astronomers *observed* the supernova *explode*.**

Below is a list of some verbs that are useful in scientific writing:

1. Verbs followed by infinitives:

learn	manage	expect	appear
prepare	arrange	fail	encourage
plan	agree	neglect	inspire
decide	offer	refuse	tend
determine	hope	seem	help

2. Verbs followed by infinitives without *to*:

Modals		Verbs of the Senses*		Other Verbs
can	will	see	watch	let
could	would	hear	observe	make
may	shall	feel	notice	help
might	should			
must				

3. Verbs followed by gerunds:

stop	deny	consider
finish	delay	involve
admit	postpone	risk
avoid	anticipate	keep
resist	suggest	prevent

4. Verbs followed by either infinitives with *to* or gerunds:

begin	permit	choose
start	allow	prefer
continue	remember	intend
try	forget	like
attempt	regret	propose

A good way to master these verb forms is to practice using them in short phrases until their correct use becomes a habit:

I can go, I could go, I may go, I might go, I will go
I learned to drive, I prepared to drive, I planned to drive
We stopped studying, we finished studying, we avoided studying

Choosing Verb Forms.   Circle the letter of the correct form of the verb in each of these sentences.

1. The monitoring device could _____ alpha particles in the atmosphere.
   a. detect   b. to detect

2. Metals are called reducing agents because they tend _____ electrons.
   a. losing   b. to lose

3. We expected _____ the thunder after we saw the lightning.
   a. hearing   b. to hear

*These verbs can also be followed by a gerund. For example, *We saw the baby birds hatching in their nest. The inhabitants could feel the earth trembling.*

4. The wound stopped _____ when pressure was applied.
   a. bleeding   b. to bleed

5. Some scientists believe that life might _____ on Saturn's moon Titan.
   a. exist   b. to exist

6. Galileo's work inspired Newton _____ motion.
   a. to study   b. studying

7. We felt the house _____ when the train went by.
   a. vibrating   b. to vibrate

8. Many animals would _____ extinct if they were not bred in captivity.
   a. become   b. becoming

9. The cafeteria only allows students _____ in certain areas.
   a. smoke   b. to smoke

10. In the 1920s, evidence began _____ that all galaxies were rushing away
    from ours.
    a. to indicate   b. indicate

READING SKILLS

Vocabulary Building

Like prefixes and suffixes, word roots can help you acquire and remember new words. The root of a word (sometimes called the *stem*) is the base from which it is formed. The root is the part most likely to give you a clue to the meaning of the word. An English word may be built from one or more roots, with or without prefixes, suffixes, or both. Here are some examples:

synchronize—**to happen at the same time**
   syn- **(prefix meaning** *together* **or** *with*)
   -chrono- **(root meaning** *time*)
   -ize **(suffix indicating verb)**

dissonance—**unpleasant sound**
   dis- **(prefix meaning** *not*)
   -son- **(root meaning** *sound*)
   -ance **(suffix indicating noun)**

photoelectric—**pertaining to the emission of electrons when a substance is exposed to light**
   photo- **(root meaning** *light*)
   -electro- **(root meaning** *electricity*)
   -ic **(suffix indicating adjective)**

Note that in all the above examples, the root is the part of the word that gives the strongest clue to its meaning. The prefix modifies or adds to the meaning of the root. The suffix indicates the part of speech (noun, verb, adjective, or adverb).

The word roots taught in this book are commonly found in scientific words. After a while, these and other roots will become familiar as you see them again and again.

Word Roots: **bio-, aero-, thermo-, hydro-.**   Study the following list of word roots and then match the terms at the left below with their meanings at the right. You will not use all the meanings listed.

bio-: **life;**
biology = **the study of living things**

aero-: **air;**
aeronautics = **the science of operating aircraft**

thermo-: **heat;**
thermometer = **a device for measuring heat**

hydro-: **water;**
hydroelectricity = **electricity produced by water power**

_____*e*_____ 1. biochemistry

_____ 2. biosynthesis

_____ 3. aerodynamics

_____ 4. aerobe

_____ 5. thermostat

_____ 6. thermodynamics

_____ 7. hydrous

_____ 8. hydraulic

_____ 9. dehydration

a. instrument for measuring specific gravity

b. device for regulating indoor temperature

c. study of the movement of air and other gases

d. use of water pressure for mechanical means

e. study of the composition of plants and animals

f. containing water

g. process of losing water

h. combination of elements by a living thing

i. organism that lives only in the presence of oxygen (air)

j. study of the conversion of heat into mechanical energy and the reverse

Vocabulary in Context.   Circle the letter of the answer that best matches the meaning of the italicized word as it is used in each of these sentences.

1. Oil and water *repel* each other.
   a. attract   (b.) resist

2. The possibility of life existing elsewhere in the universe is *intriguing* to many scientists.
   a. ridiculous   b. interesting

3. Marie and Pierre Curie were able to *isolate* a new radioactive element, radium.
   a. separate   b. create

4. The bridge was *suspended* from cables supported by towers at either end.
   a. hung   b. separated

5. The hands on the dial *pivoted* as the gas pressure was raised and lowered.
   a. rotated   b. reversed

6. The blueprint for the machinery was *accurate* except for one error.
   a. correct   b. incorrect

7. To make sure the names were chosen by chance, the computer was programmed to list them *at random*.
   a. without order   b. in order

8. During the eclipse, the earth, sun, and moon were *aligned*.
   a. in a line   b. out of line

9. The experiments were conducted *simultaneously* in London and Rome.
   a. in the same place   b. at the same time

Scanning

Scan the following passage in three minutes and put square brackets around the answers to these questions. (First identify the key words.)

1. Who was William Gilbert?
2. Where is the magnetic North Pole?
3. What did Michael Faraday and Joseph Henry both discover?

Reading

The Magic of a Magnet

What is the magic that enables a magnet to pick up an iron nail but not a wooden pencil, a rubber eraser, or a copper penny? Magnetism, named for the ancient Greek town of Magnesia, is a force of nature that manifests itself differently in different materials. Although every substance is magnetic to some degree, magnetic effects are much more powerful with iron and steel than with materials such as wood, rubber, copper and glass.

If you have ever played with two magnets, you know the powerful force with which certain ends are drawn toward each other and other ends push away from each other across space. The magnets' two north poles repel each other and their two south poles attract each other.

Physicists have always been intrigued by the fact that when a magnet is cut in half, two new magnets are formed, each with a north and south pole. If we were to cut these two magnets, we would have four magnets, each with a north and south pole. The north pole cannot be isolated from the south pole. Magnetic poles never exist alone.

The ability of magnetic iron ores, or lodestones, to attract iron and other substances was known to the ancient Greeks. Later, around the year 1100, the Chinese discovered that if a splinter of lodestone were suspended from a thread, it would pivot and point north and south, thus making a very accurate compass. This phenomenon was explained in 1600 by William Gilbert, Queen Elizabeth's doctor, who speculated that the earth itself was a gigantic magnet.

The earth's magnetism is one of the great mysteries of science which no one has been able to explain. Although the earth has an iron core, that core cannot be a magnet because at great heats (over 1000° C at the center of the earth) iron loses its magnetism. Another mystery is the fact that the magnetic poles are actually located over a thousand miles from the North and South Poles and they are not even at exactly opposite sides of the earth. In addition, by studying the age of rocks, scientists have discovered that from time to time in the history of the earth, the earth's magnetic field actually reverses itself as the magnetic South Pole becomes the magnetic North Pole and vice versa!

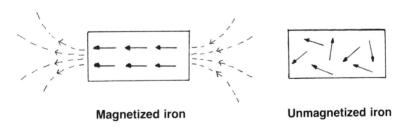

Magnetized iron   **Unmagnetized iron**

When viewed under an electron microscope, a piece of iron can be seen to be made up of many tiny magnetic areas called domains. When these domains are orderly arranged, the iron is magnetized. When these domains are randomly arranged, the iron will not act as a magnet. This explains why a magnet will pick up unmagnetized pieces of metal such as a steel paper clip. The force of the magnet causes all the tiny magnetic domains of the paper clip to align themselves. Then the north pole of the paper clip is attracted to the south pole of the magnet, and the south pole of the paper clip is attracted to the north pole of the magnet.

In 1832, the connection between magnetism and electricity was simultaneously discovered by the Englishman Michael Faraday and the American Joseph Henry.

They found that when a magnet is passed through a coil of wire, it produces an electric current in the wire. This occurs because the wire contains unattached electrons. A magnetic field moving near the wire pulls these free electrons along the wire, creating an electric current.

Not only does a moving magnetic field induce electricity, but the opposite is also true. Electric currents produce magnetism. When a current of electricity is passed through a conductor, a magnetic field forms around it. Thus a magnetic field may be induced by an electric current. Scientists believe that all magnetic fields are produced by electric currents. This is the true magic of a magnet.

Understanding the Reading.   Indicate whether each of these sentences is true (*T*) or false (*F*) according to the previous passage.

___*T*___ 1. All substances are somewhat magnetic.

_____ 2. Magnetic poles that are alike attract each other.

_____ 3. A magnet can exert its force across an open space.

_____ 4. A north pole of a magnet cannot exist separately from a south pole.

_____ 5. Compasses were used by the ancient Greeks.

_____ 6. William Gilbert suggested that a compass needle points north and south because the earth is a magnet.

_____ 7. We know that the earth is a magnet because it has an iron core.

_____ 8. The magnetic poles of the earth are located precisely at the geographical North and South Poles.

_____ 9. The earth's magnetic field reverses itself periodically.

_____ 10. A piece of iron is magnetized when its domains are scattered in different directions.

_____ 11. Metals are good electrical conductors because they contain many loose electrons.

_____ 12. Magnets can produce electricity, but electricity cannot produce magnetism.

LISTENING SKILLS

Vocabulary in Context.   Circle the letter of the answer that best matches the meaning of the italicized word as it is used in each of these sentences.

1. The astronomy class studied the sun, the moon, and other *celestial* objects.
   a. heavenly   b. imaginary

2. In 1986, a *massive* earthquake in Mexico City killed many people.
   a. huge   b. moderate

3. Benjamin Franklin noticed the *repulsion* of like electrical charges.
   a. dislike   b. attraction

4. Although a lit cigarette started the forest fire, the *underlying* cause was the lack of rainfall.
   a. immediate   b. basic

5. The policeman used a clean towel to *bind* the wound.
   a. tie   b. open

6. Californians are *aware* of the threat of earthquakes.
   a. conscious   b. ignorant

7. An atom has no charge because positive protons *cancel* negative electrons.
   a. neutralize   b. dominate

Note-Taking

   Always write clearly when taking notes, even though you use abbreviations and shortened forms of words. Keep in mind that because the subject matter is unfamiliar, it may be difficult to reread what you have written. You want to be able to concentrate on the ideas, not on figuring out what you wrote.
   Also, never waste time by copying or typing your notes. While you are copying or typing, you are *not* absorbing the material. Make the effort to write clearly the first time.
   Take notes as you listen to the lecture "The Four Forces" and then use your notes to complete the next exercise.

Understanding the Lecture.   Based on the information in the lecture, indicate whether the force described in each of these phrases is gravitational (*G*), electromagnetic (*E*), strong nuclear (*SN*), or weak nuclear (*WN*).

___*E*___ 1. The force that causes friction.

_____ 2. The weakest force.

_____   3. The most important force.

_____   4. The force that holds atoms and molecules together.

_____   5. The force that holds protons together.

_____   6. The force that sticks tape to a piece of paper.

_____   7. The force that keeps planets in orbit.

_____   8. The force that appears in radioactivity.

_____   9. The force that attracts but does not repel.

_____   10. The two forces that function only inside an atom.

_____   11. The force that is strongly felt because planets are so large.

_____   12. The contact force.

_____   13. The basic force of chemistry.

DISCUSSION POINTS

Give verbal directions to fellow students to complete some procedure. You might want to choose from the following suggestions:

1. Play a game from another country.
2. Cook a dish from another country.
3. Perform an experiment not discussed in this class.
4. Make something by hand.
5. Perform an activity such as changing the oil in a car, repairing a radio, or developing film.

Plan your talk carefully so that all necessary steps are included. A major metropolitan newspaper once printed a recipe that included a step that said to remove the chicken from the pot. Unfortunately, the step that said to *put* the chicken in the pot had accidentally been omitted. One lady wrote that she had followed the recipe carefully but was very confused when she looked in her pot for the chicken and could not find it! As you prepare your talk:

1. List all the steps in the procedure.
2. Make sure that each step is separate and distinct and that nothing has been omitted.
3. Arrange the steps in chronological order.

Your topic sentence will be a statement of the purpose of your talk. A good way to conclude is to explain how this information might be used.

WRITING SKILLS

Directions

In a science fiction story by the American writer Isaac Asimov, two astronauts on a mission far from earth are unable to operate their space station because they cannot understand the written instructions for assembling the equipment. When they notify earth of their predicament, they are told they will receive a robot that can follow the instructions and assemble the equipment. At last the box arrives. They open it excitedly only to find the robot in 500 separate pieces with one page of confusing instructions on how to assemble it!

The moral of this story is, of course, to make sure your written directions are clear. The following are guidelines for writing directions:

1. List all the steps in the process.
2. Begin each step with an imperative verb.
3. Arrange the steps in strict chronological order.
4. Keep the sentences fairly short. (Do not put more than one step together.)
5. Include all necessary details, such as specific quantities, measurements, and dates.
6. Check to see that you have not omitted anything or included any unnecessary steps.

Writing Directions

Following the guidelines listed above, write instructions for following a procedure to do or make something. Choose one of the Discussion Points or a topic of your own.

chapter 9

Calculating
Liquids and Gases

INTRODUCTION

To a large extent, mathematics is the language of science. The accuracy of predictions depends on the accuracy of the measurements and computations used in experimentation. We have come a long way since ancient times, when mathematics was regarded by some, like Plato, as mysterious or supernatural; when numbers like seven or thirteen were thought to have magical powers for good or bad luck; and when members of certain brotherhoods were put to death for revealing mathematical "secrets" that are common knowledge today.

Mathematics gives precision to science. Our calculations tell us, for example, not merely that light travels fast but that it travels at a speed of 186,000 miles per second. We know not just that bacteria are so small that they are invisible but also that several hundred thousand bacteria could fit on the period at the end of this sentence. Scientists calculate everything from the number of atoms in a gram of hydrogen to the heat of the sun; from the width of a galaxy of stars to the number of calories in a granola bar; and from the date when living things first appeared on the earth to the time when our sun will expire.

Short Reading

Read the following passage to find sentences that express mathematical relationships.

Pressure: As Molecules Collide

Everything around us is made of atoms—the earth, our bodies, the sea, the air. Small groups of atoms form molecules. In gases, the molecules are loosely attached and move about bumping into each other and into any surface they touch. This constant drumming of the molecules on a surface is called pressure.

The gas we are most familiar with is air. Since gases expand to fill any container, you might wonder why our air does not escape into outer space. The answer is simply that gravity holds the atmosphere close to the earth. In fact, due to the gravitational pull, the gases of our atmosphere accumulate near the surface of the earth. Air gets progressively thinner the higher you go, until it gradually disappears into space. Because the air is so thin at very high elevations, such as the Himalaya Mountains, climbers take oxygen to help them breathe.

The ancient Greeks knew that air had substance, that is, that it was not merely empty space, because they could feel the wind or their exhaled breath. Galileo proved that air actually has weight. Under normal climatic conditions, the weight of the air at sea level is equal to 14.7 pounds per square inch. This means that the

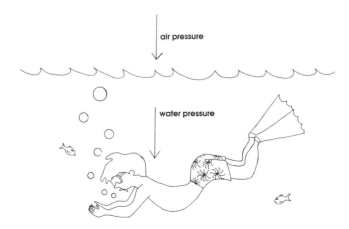

air in a medium-sized room may weigh more than one hundred pounds! Why don't we feel this enormous pressure on our bodies? The reason is that atmospheric pressure is universal; it acts in all directions on all surfaces so that everything on the earth is in balance.

The pressure inside your body equals the pressure outside. When you go up in an elevator or airplane, you feel your ears popping because as the air gets thinner, the number of molecules "hammering" inside your ear exceeds the number "hammering" outside, until the molecules have a chance to equalize.

Because the molecules are closer together in a liquid than in a gas, they slip and slide over and around each other, exerting pressure on the walls of their container. You feel this pressure when you dive beneath the surface of the water. The pressure of the water is directly proportional to the depth. The pressure on a diver is thus equal to the weight of the atmospheric pressure plus the water pressure.

USING ENGLISH TO CALCULATE

Mathematical relationships can be expressed in sentences using phrases like *is equal to, is proportional to,* and *is the product of.*

. . . the weight of the air at sea level is equal to 14.7 pounds per square inch.

$$\text{weight} = \frac{14.7 \text{ pounds}}{1 \text{ square inch}}$$

The pressure inside your body equals the pressure outside.

$$\text{pressure}^1 = \text{pressure}^2$$

The pressure on a diver is thus equal to the weight of the atmospheric pressure plus the water pressure.

$$\text{pressure on diver} = \text{atmospheric pressure} + \text{water pressure}$$

The pressure of the water is directly proportional to the depth.

$$\text{water pressure} \propto \text{depth}$$

Note: Mathematical relationships are expressed in the present tense because they are universals. They usually contain the verb *to be.*

Understanding Mathematical Terms.   The science of physics is concerned largely with the measurement of such physical quantities as length, time, and volume. Many of these quantities are related. Each of the following sentences expresses a mathematical relationship. Using letters as symbols, write a formula for each re-lationship.

1. Work is the product of force times the distance through which the force acts.

   $$w = f \times d$$

2. Velocity is calculated by dividing distance by time.
3. The volume of a cube is calculated by multiplying the length times the width times the height.
4. Power is the rate in which work is done; it is computed by dividing work by time.
5. Kinetic energy is calculated as one-half the product of the mass times the velocity squared.
6. The circumference of a circle equals pi (π) times the diameter.
7. Degrees Celsius equal five-ninths times degrees Fahrenheit minus thirty-two.

Indefinite Articles

For students of English as a second language, the use of the articles may be very confusing. The indefinite articles (*a* and *an*)* are used differently in English than in some languages. The most important rules are:

1. Plural nouns never take the indefinite article.

   A seismograph is a device for measuring an earthquake.
   (singular)
   Seismographs are devices for measuring earthquakes.
   (plural)

2. Some nonplural nouns take indefinite articles and some do not. Nouns that are countable in English take indefinite articles when they are singular. Nouns that are not countable in English do *not* take indefinite articles.

   a telescope, an electrode, a leaf (countable)
   copper, chemistry, oil, pollution (not countable)

3. Some nouns used frequently in scientific writing can be countable or not countable, depending on how they are used.

   sound (in general) **or a sound** (a particular sound)
   glass (the substance) **or a glass** (the kind we drink from)
   color (in general) **or a color** (such as red or blue)

*a is used before consonant sounds (*a* book); *an* is used before vowel sounds (*an* atom, *an* honor).

Using Indefinite Articles.   Insert an indefinite article (*a* or *an*) whenever necessary in the following sentences. Not every blank needs an article.

1. Sir Alexander Fleming discovered _____ penicillin, __*a*__ drug that is obtained from mold and used for curing _____ diseases.

2. It is thought that _____ quasar may be _____ galaxy that is exploding.

3. In comparison, _____ zinc is _____ moderately active metal.

4. We know today that _____ heat is _____ energy.

5. There was insufficient _____ light in the laboratory, so we installed _____ extra fluorescent light.

6. Electric irons are not made of _____ iron, and _____ glasses are not always made of _____ glass.

7. Radioactive substances emit _____ alpha rays, _____ beta rays, and _____ gamma rays.

8. Oxygen is _____ colorless, odorless, and tasteless gas.

Definite Articles

The definite article (*the*) may be used with plural nouns and with either countable or uncountable single nouns. Some common uses of the definite article in scientific English are:

1. to specify or refer to something that has already been mentioned (Notice that *the* is used the second and all succeeding times a noun is mentioned.)

> **In 1986 there was an accident at a nuclear reactor in Chernobyl in the Soviet Union, causing the spread of dangerous radiation. The reactor was shut down. The accident awakened concern for the safety of nuclear reactors all over the world.**

2. to refer to something that is unique

> **a planet, the earth**
> **an era, the Middle Ages**

3. to refer to something specific

> **The doctor performed an operation.** (general)
> **The doctor performed the bone marrow transplant operation he was famous for.** (specific)

4. to express superlatives

the heaviest element, the most difficult task

5. with ordinal numbers (first, second, third, fourth, last, and the like)

the nineteenth century
the ninety-fourth element
the last eclipse

6. with a noun that is followed by an *of* phrase

the theory of relativity
the atomic number of oxygen
the discovery of penicillin

Note: The definite article is never used with names of people and is only used with the names of certain places.

Using Definite Articles.   Insert *a, an*, or *the* whenever necessary in these sentences. Not every blank needs an article.

1. __*A*__ biochemistry professor wanted to do __*an*__ experiment on

_____ guinea pigs. __*The*__ experiment was never performed because

__*the*__ professor could not obtain __*the*__ animals he needed.

2. _____ Humber Bridge in Great Britain is _____ longest suspension

bridge in _____ world.

3. Some astronomers sighted _____ comet, but it was not _____ comet they

expected to see.

4. In 1946, _____ Eckert and _____ Mauchly designed _____ first

all-electronic computer.

5. _____ effect of radiation on _____ living things depends on _____

amount of radiation absorbed and _____ rate of absorption.

READING SKILLS

Vocabulary Building

Once you have learned the meaning of a word, make an effort to memorize it. Don't try to study from long lists of words; words need to be absorbed in small doses on an ongoing basis. First choose the words you want to remember: words that recur often, those used in your field of study, and others that you know will be useful in your general vocabulary. Then write three to five of these words on an index card or piece of paper. Write the meaning of each word and a phrase that shows you how to use it and will provide a meaningful association:

chronic—lasting a long time; a chronic illness

Carry the card or paper with you and use spare moments to review the words. Make sentences with each word or think about how you would use it. When you have mastered the words on your card, repeat the process. Keep the old cards at home and review them from time to time.

Number Prefixes.   Study the following list of prefixes and then match the terms at the left below with their meanings at the right. You will not use all the meanings listed.

uni-/mono-	= 1
duo-/di-/bi-	= 2
tri-	= 3
quad-/tetra-	= 4
penta-	= 5
hexa-	= 6
octa-	= 8
deci-	= $\frac{1}{10}$
deca-	= 10
centi-	= 100 or $\frac{1}{100}$
milli-	= $\frac{1}{1000}$
kilo-	= 1000

_____*d*_____ 1. binary

_____ 2. pentagon

_____ 3. trigonometry

_____ 4. hexangular

_____ 5. diameter

_____ 6. deciliter

_____ 7. decaliter

_____ 8. monochrome

_____ 9. kilogram

_____ 10. milligram

a. study of right triangles

b. having 4 sides

c. line that cuts a circle in half

d. involving 2

e. having 6 angles

f. single color

g. five-sided figure

h. 1000 grams

i. $\frac{1}{1000}$ of a gram

j. 10 liters

k. $\frac{1}{10}$ of a liter

Vocabulary in Context.   Circle the letter of the answer that best matches the meaning of the italicized word as it is used in each of these sentences.

1. The temperature on a Fahrenheit fever thermometer *ranges* from 94° to 108°.
   a. extends   b. contracts

2. Swimmers feel more *buoyant* in salt water than in fresh water.
   a. floatable   b. sinkable

3. The television viewers *observed* the explosion of the space shuttle.
   a. watched   b. heard

4. Word processors have *displaced* typewriters in many offices.
   a. taken the place of   b. damaged

5. The frog quickly became *immersed* in the water and could no longer be seen.
   a. submerged   b. protected

6. The *volume* of air in a room can be measured in cubic feet.
   a. quality   b. quantity

7. Ten *minus* four equals six.
   a. less   b. plus

8. The *degree* of gravitational pull depends on the size of the objects involved.
   a. quality   b. amount

9. The *density* of the fog gave us poor visibility.
   a. thickness   b. coolness

10. Newton *computed* the weights of the planets.
    a. measured   b. calculated

11. Water contains hydrogen and oxygen in a *ratio* of two to one.
    a. proportion   b. size

Scanning

Scan the following passage in three minutes and put square brackets around the answers to these questions. (First identify the key words.)

1. What is Archimedes' principle?
2. What type of water has a density of 64 pounds per cubic foot?
3. What is the specific gravity of people?

Note: Key words may include words that do not appear in the question. For example, key words for the third question might include *human beings* or *man* as well as *people* and *specific gravity*.

Reading

What Makes Objects Float?

As a child, you may have played with objects in the bathtub, noticing that the bar of soap sank to the bottom of the water while the plastic soap dish floated on top. Why is it that many objects, ranging from a piece of cork to an ocean liner, will float, while others will not?

The force that makes objects float is called buoyancy. This concept was established by the great Greek mathematician Archimedes, who also played in the bathtub. Archimedes observed that when he got into his bathtub, water was displaced, or pushed out. He determined that any object immersed in a liquid is buoyed up by a force equal to the weight of the fluid displaced by the object. This is known as Archimedes' principle. For example, suppose a rock weighs 100 pounds and has a volume of 1 cubic foot. When that rock is submerged in water, it displaces 1 cubic foot of water, which weighs 62 pounds. Therefore, the gravitational pull on the rock is 100 pounds downward and the buoyant force is 62 pounds upward. Out of the water, you would need to exert a force of 100 pounds to lift the rock. In the water you would have to exert a force of 100 minus 62 pounds (or 38 pounds).

The buoyant force of a liquid, or how much it pushes upward, depends on the density of the liquid. A body will float if its density is less than that of the liquid in which it is immersed; it will sink if its density is greater. Ice is less dense than water, so icebergs float on the surface of the ocean. Steel ships are designed with many spaces filled with air so that their density is less than that of water.

Density is computed by dividing the weight of the liquid by its volume. Saltwater has a density of 64 pounds per cubic foot, while fresh water has a density of 62 pounds per cubic foot. Hence the buoyant force of saltwater is greater than that of fresh water, which explains why it is easier for a swimmer to float in the ocean than in a lake. Similarly, an ice cube will float in a glass of water. That same ice cube would sink in pure alcohol, because alcohol has a lower density than ice. The tendency of an ice cube to sink or float in a drink depends on the proportion of water to alcohol. Be on your guard if you put an ice cube in a drink and it sinks to the bottom!

Specific gravity is the ratio of the density of a substance to the density of water. Human beings have a specific gravity of approximately 1.0, which is the same as that of water. This is not surprising, considering that our bodies are two-thirds water! However, a fat person has less specific gravity than a thin person and therefore will have an easier time floating.

Drawing Conclusions.   After reading the previous passage carefully, indicate what conclusions can be drawn from the information it contains by circling the letter of the answer that better completes each of the following sentences.

1. A small rock will _____ .
   a. float better than a large one   b. not float better than a large one

2. If a ship weighs more than 64 pounds per cubic foot, it will _____ .
   a. sink   b. float

3. Since cork floats in water, we know that its density is _____ .
   a. more than that of water   b. less than that of water

4. It is easier to float if you are _____ .
   a. thin   b. fat

5. A ship will float higher in _____ .
   a. lake water   b. ocean water

6. The best place to make a scientific discovery is _____ .
   a. in the bathtub   b. not stated in the passage

7. An egg will float better in _____ .
   a. salt water   b. fresh water

8. At a party, if an ice cube sinks to the bottom of your drink you should _____ .
   a. go home   b. investigate the contents of the drink

9. It is easy to lift someone in the water because of the _____ .
   a. buoyant force   b. specific gravity

10. Archimedes must have been _____ .
    a. a clever Greek mathematician   b. very clean

LISTENING SKILLS

Vocabulary in Context. Circle the letter of the answer that best matches the meaning of the italicized word as it is used in each of these sentences.

1. The weather was *a factor* in the decision to cancel the space flight.
   a. a reason   b. an event

2. A frog or turtle can live in either a land or sea *environment*.
   a. temperature   b. surroundings

3. A moving object will continue to move *provided* no force such as friction acts on it.
   a. as long as   b. in order that

4. The monkeys were *confined to* a small cage.
   a. enclosed in   b. released from

5. The price of gasoline was *quadrupled*, and there were fears it would go even higher.
   a. multiplied by four   b. divided by four

6. Newton's discoveries *affected* the philosophy and science of Western civilization for several centuries.
   a. influenced   b. disproved

7. A scientific analysis must be *quantitative* to be precise.
   a. mathematical   b. massive

8. All the *implications* of the atomic explosion at Hiroshima are still not known.
   a. causes   b. effects

9. The *converse* of evaporation is condensation.
   a. reverse   b. effect.

10. In bright light, the pupils of your eyes *contract*.
    a. expand   b. shrink

11. Success was *attained* after numerous experiments.
    a. denied   b. achieved

12. Absolute proof of some concepts is *unattainable*.
    a. not desirable   b. not possible

Note-Taking

It is always a good idea to read over your notes as soon as possible following a lecture. Students taking notes frequently complain that the instructor talks too fast. If you are having trouble keeping up with the instructor, leave spaces in your notebook as you take notes. After the lecture add to your notes details that are still fresh in your mind. Also correct anything that you didn't write down clearly in your haste. Ask questions to clarify anything you don't understand before the class moves on to the next topic and you become lost. Also, when you hear an unfamiliar word that is important to the lecture and you cannot guess its meaning, write it phonetically (the way it sounds), circle it, and later ask your instructor what it means or find it in the dictionary as soon as you have an opportunity.

Take notes as you listen to the lecture "The Remarkable Behavior of Gases." Then use your notes to complete the next exercise.

Understanding the Lecture.   Indicate whether each of the following statements is true (*T*) or false (*F*) according to the information in the lecture. Use your notes to help you.

_____*T*_____ 1. The behavior of gases is subject to changes in temperature, pressure, and volume.

_____ 2. If you've seen one gas behave, you've seen them all.

_____ 3. The first gas law was discovered by Avogadro.

_____ 4. The volume of a gas is inversely proportional to the pressure.

_____ 5. Only certain gases expand when heated.

_____ 6. Charles discovered that the volume of a gas is directly related to its temperature.

_____ 7. Charles' experiments proved that at $-273°$ C, the volume of a gas will shrink to nothing.

_____ 8. Avogadro's Law is referred to as the molecular hypothesis.

_____ 9. Equal volumes of all gases contain the same number of molecules.

_____ 10. At lower temperatures, molecules require more space to move around.

_____ 11. Lord Kelvin proposed that at $-273°$ C it is the energy of the molecules, not the volume of a gas, that is reduced to zero.

_____ 12. A temperature of $-273°$ C is good weather for skiing.

_____ 13. It was not until recently that physicists were able to attain a temperature of absolute zero.

DISCUSSION POINTS

1. What are some things that a biologist needs to calculate? an astronomer? a chemist? a physicist? a geologist?
2. What could you measure or calculate in your classroom? (Think beyond linear measurements to such things as weight, volume, temperature, size and humidity.)
3. Some people have suggested that we use the decimal system because we have ten fingers. Suppose we had the same number of limbs as an octopus or a three-toed sloth? What kind of numbering system do you think we might have?
4. The ancient Hindus developed the concept of zero, which was later adopted by the Arabs. Why was that concept so important?
5. Why do you think some ancient people believed mathematics to be mysterious? Why do you think certain numbers were considered magical, that is, lucky or unlucky?

WRITING SKILLS

Parallel Form

Whenever you have a list of items, it is preferable to write them in parallel form, that is, with all the items in the same format. For example, the sentence *Ellen likes to paint, swimming, and dance* is unacceptable. The same sentence may be written three different ways, using parallel form. Notice how each of these examples is smoother, clearer, and easier to read than the original sentence:

Ellen likes painting, swimming, and dancing.
Ellen likes to paint, to swim, and to dance.
Ellen likes to paint, swim, and dance.

Similarly, in any paragraph there should be some consistency or regularity in tense and person. Decide if the past, present, or future tense is most appropriate and use that tense throughout. Then decide if you are going to write in the first person (*I* or *we*), second person (*you*), or third person (*he, she, it, they, John,* and so on).

Look at the following example of how *not* to write:

I filled a one-quart container with water. Then dissolve half a cup of salt in the water. The salt was stirred until it was dissolved.

The paragraph is confusing because it mixes tenses; first, second, and third person; and passive and active voice. Notice how much clearer the paragraph becomes when there is consistency, or parallelism:

Fill a one-quart container with water. Then dissolve half a cup of salt in the water. Stir the salt until it dissolves.

Writing More Directions

Write a paragraph giving directions for one of the following. Be specific about each step in the process, that is, indicate what needs to be measured, recorded, or multiplied. Make sure all steps are in chronological order. To give your paragraph parallel form, use the imperative form of the verb.

1. How to calculate the weight of an elephant.

2. How to calculate the difference between the amount of time you spend studying and the amount of time you spend watching television in a week.
3. How to calculate the speed (miles or kilometers per hour) of a flight from Paris to Tokyo.
4. How to calculate the height of a tree.
5. How to calculate the percent of your weekly expenses that goes toward recreation.
6. How to calculate what it would cost you to drive from New York to San Francisco.

chapter 10

Reporting
The Origin of Life

INTRODUCTION

Throughout history, human beings have made many discoveries about themselves and their environment. However, modern science did not really begin until people started reporting their observations and discoveries and communicating their ideas. This was not always done. In ancient Greece, a secret society of mathematicians, known as the Pythagoreans, hid their findings from the world. In the Middle Ages, the alchemists went to great lengths to conceal their discoveries. Today, scientists report their findings and detail their experimental methods in journals, inviting others to perform experiments to verify or disprove the results. Each discovery suggests new paths of investigation, leading to the increasingly rapid expansion of scientific knowledge.

Most discoveries are not accomplished by one person but by a sharing or exchange of information with researchers building on each other's work. The development of atomic energy, for example, was based on the work of Albert Einstein, Niels Bohr, Enrico Fermi, and many other scientists in Europe and America. The development of the computer and the project that put a man on the moon are other examples of great scientific achievements that were joint efforts. This type of cooperation is dependent upon intelligent, accurate reporting.

Short Reading

Read the following passage and notice the different verb tenses that are used to report events of the past.

How Life Began

To discover how life began, archaeologists study fossils. Fossils are the remains or imprints of plants and animals of long ago that have been preserved in the earth's crust. The simplest forms of life appear in the lowest or oldest rocks. Although scientists can calculate that the earth is 4.6 billion years old, the oldest rocks that show any trace of life are less than 2 billion years old. Therefore, about 2.5 billion years had passed on the earth when life originated. Since the oldest forms of life were all sea life, many scientists believe life began in the sea.

We do not know exactly how, but in some miraculous way, the right kind of molecules happened to combine in the ocean or in clay to form a minute organism. All life has probably evolved from that single original cell, which may have been something like the bacteria of today. This one-celled organism ate, grew, responded to its surroundings, reproduced itself, and spread throughout the oceans.

Probably those first tiny organisms were not all alike. Some were better able to obtain food or adapt to colder waters. The stronger cells survived and their characteristics were passed on to the next generation.

The early cells reproduced simply by dividing in two. After a long time, single cells became attached to one another, and each cell became specialized in a different function. Gradually organisms became more and more complex. Today, many living things are made up of a combination of cells; our bodies are composed of skin cells, blood cells, muscle cells, brain cells, and so on.

The gradual migration of life from the ocean to the land was another major step that made many advances possible. Eventually plants and animals divided into males and females, and possibilities increased for developing new and varied species or types. To date, more than 400,000 species of plants and 1,200,000 species of animals have developed. Gradually, the senses of sight and hearing improved in animals and brains grew and developed. Finally, intelligence progressed, leading to the development of human beings.

USING ENGLISH TO REPORT

Different tenses are used to report past actions. The simple past tense is the most frequently used in scientific writing.

A COMPLETED ACTION

This one-celled organism ate, grew, responded to its surroundings, reproduced itself, and spread throughout the oceans.
(These actions have taken place a long time ago and are completed.)

Simple past tense: **ate, grew, responded, reproduced, spread**

Probably those first tiny organisms were not all alike.
(This sentence reports a condition rather than an action.)

Simple past tense: **were**

. . . their characteristics were passed onto the next generation.
(The passive form is used because the action is more important than the performer of the action.)

Simple past tense, passive form: **were passed**

AN UNCOMPLETED ACTION

To date, more than 400,000 species of plants and 1,200,000 species of animals have developed.
(This is an action that has taken place over a period of time, is taking place now, and will probably continue into the future.)

Present perfect tense: **have developed**

All life has probably evolved from that single original cell. . . .
(This action is also incomplete, that is, life is still evolving.)

Present perfect tense: **has evolved**

AN ACTION COMPLETED BEFORE A GIVEN PAST TIME

Therefore, about 2.5 billion years had passed on the earth when life originated.

Past perfect tense: **had passed**

Sentence Patterns

REPORTING A COMPLETED ACTION (SIMPLE PAST TENSE)

Darwin { published / announced / proposed } his theory of evolution in 1859.

REPORTING AN UNCOMPLETED OR RECENT ACTION
(PRESENT PERFECT TENSE)

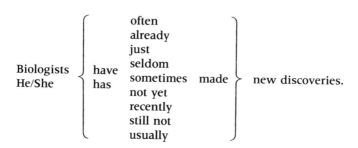

Biologists / He/She { have / has } { often / already / just / seldom / sometimes / not yet / recently / still not / usually } made { new discoveries.

REPORTING AN ACTION COMPLETED BEFORE A GIVEN TIME
(PAST PERFECT TENSE)

By the time we {arrived}, the bomb {had exploded.}
By 1957, Russia {had launched} the first Sputnik.

REPORTING A CONTINUOUS ACTION (PAST CONTINUOUS, PRESENT PERFECT
CONTINUOUS, AND PAST PERFECT CONTINUOUS TENSES)

Darwin {was working} on his theory while in the Galapagos.

The universe {has been expanding} { for 15 billion years. / since its inception. }

Darwin {had been riding} in his carriage when the idea came to him.

NOTES: *When reporting, remember the following:*
1. *Adverbs of time and frequency (such as* often, already, *and* usually) *are usually used with the present perfect tense.*
2. *The continuous past tenses are included above for reference. However, they are not discussed in the chapter because they do not occur frequently in scientific writing.*

Identifying Past Tenses.   Read the paragraph and then complete the following exercise.

THE CELL

(1) It is one of the amazing facts of science that all living organisms, from simple plants and animals to human beings, are made of cells, and that these cells are remarkably similar in structure. (2) Cells are composed of a jellylike substance called cytoplasm, with a nucleus that is the control center.

(3) The nucleus contains a large amount of nucleic acid: DNA (deoxyribonucleic acid) and RNA (ribonucleic acid). (4) For years biologists studied the nature of nucleic acid. (5) By 1953, a theory regarding the structure of the DNA molecule had been formulated by James Watson and Francis Crick. (6) They said that DNA is the information-storing molecule and that RNA is the information-carrying molecule.

(7) Cells reproduce by dividing in half to form two identical daughter cells in a process called mitosis. (8) Every living thing—a dolphin, an ant, a daisy, or a human body—has begun life as a single cell with a few molecules of DNA.

1. Write the number of a sentence that reports a completed action. _____

    a. What tense is used? _____

    b. Is it in the active or passive form? _____

2. Write the number of a sentence that reports an incomplete action. _____

    a. What tense is used? _____

    b. Is it in the passive or active form? _____

3. Write the number of a sentence that reports an action that occurs before a specific time in the past. _____

    a. What tense is used? _____

    b. Is it in the passive or active form? _____

Using the Simple Past Tense.   Each of these sentences describes a completed action. Insert either the active or passive form of the simple past tense of the verb in parentheses. A sentence is *active* if the subject *performs* the action; it is *passive* if the subject *receives* the action.

1. Charles Darwin _____*wrote*_____ (write) *The Origin of Species.*

2. The first fossils _____ (find) on rocks that are 2 billion years old.

3. The first man _____ (appear) about 1.5 million years ago.

4. About 165 million years ago, giant dinosaurs _____ (live) on the earth.

5. About 4.6 billion years ago, the earth _____ (form).

6. The first living organisms _____ (reproduce) by dividing in half.

7. The fossils of Neanderthal man _____ (discover) in Iraq between 1953 and 1960.

8. About 18 million years ago, violent earthquakes along California's San Andreas Fault _____ (rotate) the northwestern Mojave Desert about 25° clockwise.

The Present Perfect Tense

To describe an incomplete or recently completed action, the present perfect tense is used. The formulas for forming present perfect tense are:

ACTIVE

= *has* or *have* + **past participle**

PASSIVE

= *has* or *have* + *been* + **past participle**

Using the Present Perfect Tense.   Each of these sentences describes an incomplete or recently completed action. Insert either the passive or active form of the present perfect tense of the verb or verb phrase in parentheses.

1. Air pollution _____*has become*_____ (become) a major problem in our cities.

2. Many studies _____*have been made*_____ (make) to determine the effects of smog on the lungs.

3. More than a hundred elements _____ (discover).

4. A cure _____ (still not find) for the common cold.

5. A satellite of the planet Pluto _____ (recently discover).

6. Another man-made satellite _____ (just go) into orbit.

7. For many years, scientists _____ (know) there is no life on the moon.

8. Halley's Comet _____ (see) regularly every seventy-six years.

9. Human beings _____ (destroy) more living things than any other organism.

Choosing Tenses

Choosing the Correct Past Tense.   Insert the correct past tense of the verbs in parentheses in the following paragraph.

SPONTANEOUS GENERATION

Aristotle _____ (believe) that frogs and snakes _____ (generate) spontaneously from mud and insects from decayed meat. This theory of spontaneous generation _____ (held) by many people including the great scientists Isaac Newton and William Harvey. Then in 1668, the Italian scientist Francesco Redi _____ (perform) an experiment to discredit this theory. He _____ (place) meat in three jars. The first jar _____ (leave) open, the second _____ (cover) with cloth, and the third _____ (cover) with paper. When the meat _____ (decay), flies _____ (attract) by the odor and _____ (lay) eggs on the meat in the open jar and on the cloth cover of the second jar. No eggs _____ (find) in the meat or on the paper covering of the third jar. The experiment _____ (demonstrate) that living things come only from other living things. Since then, scientists like Louis Pasteur and others _____ (perform) other experiments to disprove the theory of spontaneous generation.

Forming Sentences That Report.   Form a sentence reporting each of the following events.

1. birth of the first test-tube baby / England / 1978

   The first test-tube baby was born in England in 1978.

2. development of principles of geometry / Euclid / Alexandria, Egypt / 300 B.C.
3. classification of plants and animals / Carolus Linnaeus / Sweden / 1735
4. receipt of the Nobel Prize for discovery of plutonium and radium / Marie Curie / France / 1911
5. invention of printing with movable type / Pi-sheng / China / eleventh century
6. controlled nuclear fission of uranium / Enrico Fermi / Italy / 1942
7. first landing on the moon / American Project Apollo / 1969
8. discovery of circulation of blood / William Harvey / England / 1628
9. first space flight / Yuri Gagarin / Soviet Union / 1961
10. development of polio vaccine / Jonas Salk / America / 1954
11. invention of incandescent lamp / Thomas Edison / America / 1879

READING SKILLS

Vocabulary Building

Increasing your vocabulary does not have to be accomplished while sitting at a desk with papers, books, and pencils. If you carry a card or sheet of notepaper listing four or five new words, you can take advantage of five or ten minutes you have while waiting in a line at the bank or in an office, riding a bus, or even waiting for television commercials to end. Frequent short study periods will be more productive than one weekly session with a long list.

To study the words, first read each one and its meaning. (Check with a dictionary or a native speaker if you are uncertain about pronunciation.) Then, make five sentences with the word or invent an imaginary conversation in which you would use the word. This technique will increase not only your vocabulary but also your fluency by providing you with an opportunity to practice "speaking" even when you have no one to talk with. Consider the way many people (even native speakers!) prepare themselves for a job interview or an argument with a teacher or boss by thinking through what they plan to say. When the time for the conversation comes, they are able to express themselves more effectively because they have already formulated the words in their mind. As a nonnative speaker, you will benefit from this habit of "practice talking" immeasurably. In other words, talk to yourself! (But be sure to do it in English!)

Word Roots: **photo-, chrono-, dyna-, helio-.**   Study the following list of word roots and then match the terms at the left below with their meanings at the right. You will not use all the meanings listed.

photo-: **light**
photography = **taking pictures using the action of light**

chrono-: **time**
chronology = **arrangement in order of time**

dyna-: **power**
dynamic = **energetic**

helio-: **the sun**
heliotrope = **plant that turns toward the sun**

_____c_____ 1. photon

_____ 2. photoelectric cell

_____ 3. chronometer

_____ 4. chronic

_____ 5. dynamo

_____ 6. heliocentric

_____ 7. dynamite

_____ 8. helium

a. machine that produces electric energy

b. instrument for measuring time

c. particle of light

d. relating to the center of the sun or to the sun as the center of the universe

e. vacuum tube with electrical properties modified by light

f. continuing for a long time

g. high energy explosive

h. gaseous element first seen in the sun's atmosphere

i. device for measuring the sun

Vocabulary in Context.   Circle the letter of the answer that best matches the meaning of the italicized word as it is used in each of these sentences.

1. Efforts are being made to *preserve* clean air in the cities.
   (a.) protect   b. destroy

2. The factory *generates* electricity for the entire surrounding area.
   a. produces   b. obtains

3. Although Aristotle's theories of motion were believed to be true for centuries, they were *discredited* by Galileo's experiments.
   a. supported   b. disproved

4. Numerous *species* of animals are in danger of becoming extinct.
   a. classes   b. habitats

5. The *evolution* in computer technology has accelerated since 1980.
   a. development   b. decline

6. After the bombing, the city was rebuilt by those who *survived*.
   a. lived   b. died

7. It started to rain when the air was *saturated* with moisture.
   a. filled   b. cleaned

8. Galileo discovered the *existence* of Jupiter's moons.
   a. presence   b. disappearance

9. The camel is *adapted* to desert life and can go without water for long periods.
   a. unsuited   b. adjusted

10. Einstein's theories have *prevailed* throughout the twentieth century.
    a. failed   b. dominated

11. A butterfly *evolves* from a caterpillar.
    a. escapes   b. develops

12. The subject of abortion has been *controversial* for a long time, and there will probably never be complete agreement.
    a. interesting   b. disputed

13. Newton performed experiments to *confirm* what Galileo had proposed about motion.
    a. verify   b. disprove

Skimming

Skim the following passage in three minutes or less and then answer these questions:

1. The main topic of this passage is _____ .

   a. the search to discover how human life evolved

   b. Aristotle's view of evolution

   c. the life of Charles Darwin

   d. the sex life of an oyster

2. You will find information about all of the following *except* _____ .

   a. how Darwin formulated his theory

   b. why Darwin's theory was so controversial

   c. the biblical story of the origin of man

   d. the meaning of "survival of the fittest"

Reading

Evolution

Life comes only from other life. The offspring of a living thing resembles its parents. A bird is hatched from an egg produced by parent birds. A flower grows from seeds created by a parent flower. One organism passes the flame of life to another in a continuing cycle, thus preserving life on the earth.

This concept is relatively new to mankind. The folklore of many parts of the world includes tales of abrupt transformations of men into animals and vice versa. In the fourth century B.C. even the great Greek philosopher Aristotle believed in the spontaneous generation of certain living creatures. It was not until 1668 that the Italian scientist Francesco Redi performed experiments that discredited his theory.

Then, in the mid-nineteenth century, biologists began to explore the question of how so many different species of plants and animals had developed. A young English naturalist named Charles Darwin traveled to the Galapagos Islands off the coast of South America. There he observed many types of creatures that he had never seen, including swimming lizards, giant land turtles that weighed several hundred pounds, and a type of penguin that lived in tropical weather. Darwin was struck by the fact that many of the animals that he saw lived nowhere else in the world. Then, on neighboring islands, he studied many different species of a group of birds called finches.

As a result of his observations, Darwin formulated a theory of the evolution of human life. He knew that many organisms produce more offspring than can actually survive. For example, an oyster can spawn 100 million eggs at a time! If all these eggs survived, the ocean would be saturated with oysters! Since all cannot survive, there is competition among the individuals in a species for food, water, warmth, and space. In the struggle for existence, only the fittest, or the ones that are best able to adapt, will prevail.

Darwin called his theory "natural selection," or the "survival of the fittest." He argued that those species that are the most fit, or the best able to compete with other species in the environment, will survive. The process of natural selection has occurred innumerable times. Animals with the warmest fur survive in cold areas. Plants that require the least amount of water survive in the desert. Fish that could adopt to life on land became the first land animals.

In 1859 Darwin published his findings in *The Origin of Species*. He claimed that man has evolved from a lower form of life and that in fact all life on the earth has developed from a single, original cell. Over millions of years, through gradual change, development, and natural selection, all the different species of life that we know today have evolved.

Darwin's ideas were very controversial, partly because they were in conflict with many religious views about the origin of mankind. In addition, many people were shocked at the idea that humans are animals and related to other forms of life. Particularly upsetting was the concept that the ancestors of human beings were related to apes or monkeys millions of years ago. But all the evidence we have today confirms Darwin's hypothesis.

Distinguishing Fact from Opinion.   It is very important to recognize the difference between fact and opinion when reading scientific material or listening to a scientific lecture. For example, it is a *fact* that the world population in 1987 was 4,975,000,000. However, it is the *opinion* of many scientists that the world population will increase by 1 billion in the next twenty-five years. It may be an educated opinion, that is, one based on past statistics and current trends, but it remains an opinion until it can be proved.

Indicate whether each of these sentences represents a fact (*F*) or an opinion (*O*). If you are unsure, try to determine whether the concept can be proved.

___*F*___ 1. Life comes only from other life.

_____ 2. There is no spontaneous generation of life.

_____ 3. Aristotle should have realized that there is no spontaneous generation.

_____ 4. Darwin was a genius.

_____ 5. Darwin stirred up a great deal of controversy.

_____ 6. Aristotle was a dummy.

_____ 7. The Galapagos Islands are near South America.

_____ 8. There were many unusual creatures on the Galapagos Islands.

_____ 9. Some lizards can swim.

_____ 10. Oysters produce many offspring.

_____ 11. Oysters are good to eat.

_____ 12. Human beings are animals.

_____ 13. The world would be a better place without oysters.

_____ 14. Creatures on earth will continue to evolve for many centuries.

_____ 15. We will never know how life began.

LISTENING SKILLS

Vocabulary in Context.   Circle the letter of the answer that best matches the meaning of the italicized word as it is used in each of these sentences.

1. Human babies *inherit* characteristics of both parents.
   a. acquire   b. reject

2. Monkeys have many human *traits*, such as the way they use their hands to peel a banana or scratch themselves.
   a. organs   b. characteristics

3. Many species that exist today will be extinct in a few *generations*.
   a. lifetimes   b. years

4. A perennial is a plant that *blooms* every year.
   a. flowers   b. dies

5. The midwestern part of the United States is sometimes called the "bread basket" because wheat and corn are the region's *dominant* crops.
   a. most important
   b. least important

6. The ocean's tides are characterized by alternating forward and *recessive* movements.
   a. rapid
   b. backward

7. The stars are too *numerous* to be counted.
   a. large
   b. abundant

8. Antoine Henri Becquerel's discovery of radiation was *significant* and paved the way for the work of Marie and Pierre Curie.
   a. important
   b. unimportant

9. The results of the experiment *substantiated* the hypothesis and were announced to the world.
   a. supported
   b. disproved

Note-Taking

Notes taken in class should be reviewed from time to time, especially before a test. The more frequently you review, the higher the percentage of the material you will retain. For example, if you review the notes three times, you may recall as much as 20 percent or 30 percent more than if you review them twice. Also, spacing those reviews will help you to remember over a long period of time. That is, for long-term recall, it is better to read the notes through once a week for three weeks than three times in one sitting.

Take notes as you listen to the lecture "The Science of Genetics" and then use your notes to complete the next exercise.

Understanding the Lecture.   Use your notes to determine whether each of the following statements is true (*T*) or false (*F*) according to the information in the lecture.

_____ *F* _____ 1. The Austrian monk Gregor Mendel performed his experiments in the seventeenth century.

_____ 2. Genetics is the study of how flowers reproduce.

_____ 3. Mendel's unique contribution was that he studied all the characteristics at one time.

_____ 4. When Mendel cross-pollinated red and white flowers, he expected to produce flowers that were pink or mixed red and white.

_____ 5. All the first-generation flowers were pink.

_____ 6. When Mendel self-pollinated the first-generation red flowers, he produced red flowers and white flowers.

_____ 7. Mendel discovered that the color red is dominant and the color white is recessive.

_____ 8. Mendel demonstrated that recessive factors become hidden and may emerge in later generations.

_____ 9. Two dark-haired parents may have a blond child because hair color is not hereditary.

_____ 10. The object of Mendel's experiments was to discover how character traits are inherited.

_____ 11. Later experiments proved that Mendel's ideas work only on garden peas.

_____ 12. The same principles that determine whether a flower is red or white determine whether you have brown eyes or blue eyes.

DISCUSSION POINTS

Suppose you heard that some human beings had landed on another planet. You know *what* happened. What else would you want to know? *Who* went? *When*? *Where* did they land? *How* did they get there? *Why* did they go? A good report will answer the questions *who, what, when, where, why,* and *how.*

Find a newspaper or magazine article describing a recent scientific development and give a brief oral report to the class. Answer as many of the above questions as you can. A good way to conclude is by explaining the significance of this new information.

WRITING SKILLS

Reporting

Newspaper writers use the technique of giving the reader the essential facts of an occurrence in the first paragraph of an article. These facts include answers to the questions *who, what, when, where, why,* and *how.* Discuss which of these questions are answered in the following paragraph.

An earthquake measuring 6.1 on the Richter scale shook Los Angeles, California, on October 1, 1987. The quake killed six people and caused over $100 million in damage, a reminder that there are hazards to as well as joys in living in sunny California along the San Andreas Fault. Seismologists are warning that the quake was only a preview of coming attractions. They predict that the "big one" will occur within the next few decades.

Writing a Report

Write a report of a scientific discovery or event. You might choose one of these:

1. the first human heart transplant or test-tube baby
2. the discovery of penicillin, x-rays, or radium
3. the first landing on the moon, Mount Everest, or the South Pole
4. the construction of the Pyramids, the Suez Canal, or the Panama Canal
5. the development of the atomic theory or the theory of relativity
6. the invention of the telephone, the computer, or the airplane

Begin by writing a topic sentence that answers the questions *who, what, when,* and *where.* The remainder of the paragraph can explain *how* or *why* or both. Your concluding sentence might tell the significance of the discovery or event.

chapter 11

Describing

The Universe

INTRODUCTION

A description serves to introduce a scientist's view of the world. It may describe conditions, results of an experiment, chemical changes, physical movements, or what is seen through a telescope or microscope. A description may also tell the characteristics or distinctive features of an object—how it looks, sounds, tastes, smells, works, or is produced.

The nature of something can be explained by describing it. For example, the concept of an atom is difficult to grasp from a definition alone, but a description of its appearance, detailing its structure and function, makes it easier to visualize.

Short Reading

Read the following passage to determine which properties of the sun and stars are described (for example, size?, position?).

The Sun and Other Stars

The sun is a star. It is a flaming ball of extremely hot gases. The surface temperature is about 11,000° F, hot enough to turn every solid to vapor, but relatively cool compared to the intense heat at the center.

Located about 93 million miles from the earth, the sun has a diameter that is approximately equal to 109 of our earths lined up like a row of beach balls, and a mass that is about 330,000 times the mass of the earth.

The sun is the original source of nearly all our energy. It is mostly made of hydrogen, although it also contains nearly every other kind of atom that exists on the earth. The sun derives its energy from a process of fusion in which hydrogen atoms are converted into helium atoms under extreme heat and pressure. This process creates a tremendous noise, but we cannot hear it because sound does not travel through empty space.

Our sun is not even especially large or bright compared to other stars. Stars vary in size from smaller than the earth to large enough to hold a good part of our solar system! The color of a star indicates its temperature. A star may be red (the coolest), yellow (like our sun), white, or blue (the hottest).

The nearest star is 4.3 light-years from the earth. A light-year is the distance light travels in one year, or about 6 million million miles (6,000,000,000,000 miles). The farthest stars are billions of light-years away. Some are so far away that if they were to blow up today, their light would continue to be seen from the earth for a million years!

Our sun is part of an enormous galaxy of 30 billion stars, called the Milky Way. In addition there are billions of galaxies within range of our telescopes and countless billions beyond. The enormity of space is quite beyond human comprehension. How exciting it is to live in an age when human beings have begun to explore that space.

USING ENGLISH TO DESCRIBE

Scientific writing includes descriptions of processes, substances, concepts, conditions, and events. The above passage describes some of the physical, functional, and chemical properties of the sun.

PHYSICAL DESCRIPTION

It is a flaming ball of extremely hot gases.

Shape: **ball**

Physical composition: **hot, flaming gases**

The surface temperature is about 11,000° F, hot enough to turn every solid to vapor, but relatively cool compared to the intense heat at the center.

Surface temperature: **11,000° F**
hot enough to turn every solid to vapor
cool compared to center

Located about 93 million miles from the earth . . . .

Position or location: **93 million miles from earth**

. . . the sun has a diameter that is approximately equal to 109 of our earths lined up like a row of beach balls, and a mass that is about 330,000 times the mass of the earth.

Diameter: **109 × earth's diameter**

Mass: **330,000 × earth's mass**

FUNCTIONAL DESCRIPTION

The sun is the original source of nearly all our energy.

Importance: **source of our energy**

CHEMICAL DESCRIPTION

It is mostly made of hydrogen, although it also contains nearly every other kind of atom that exists on the earth.

Chemical composition: **mostly hydrogen + nearly all other known atoms**

Sentence Patterns

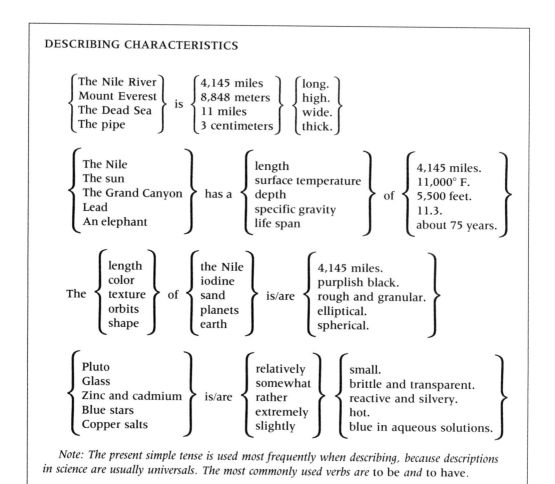

DESCRIBING CHARACTERISTICS

The Nile River / Mount Everest / The Dead Sea / The pipe — is — 4,145 miles / 8,848 meters / 11 miles / 3 centimeters — long. / high. / wide. / thick.

The Nile / The sun / The Grand Canyon / Lead / An elephant — has a — length / surface temperature / depth / specific gravity / life span — of — 4,145 miles. / 11,000° F. / 5,500 feet. / 11.3. / about 75 years.

The — length / color / texture / orbits / shape — of — the Nile / iodine / sand / planets / earth — is/are — 4,145 miles. / purplish black. / rough and granular. / elliptical. / spherical.

Pluto / Glass / Zinc and cadmium / Blue stars / Copper salts — is/are — relatively / somewhat / rather / extremely / slightly — small. / brittle and transparent. / reactive and silvery. / hot. / blue in aqueous solutions.

Note: *The present simple tense is used most frequently when describing, because descriptions in science are usually universals. The most commonly used verbs are* to be *and* to have.

Using Precise Descriptions.   Science demands objectivity and precision in its descriptions. To describe a comet as fantastic or long and beautiful tells very little. The word *fantastic* describes how you feel about something, but it does not bring an image to mind. *Long* is a relative term. Scientists need to be specific. Is it a mile long? 50 miles? 1,000 miles? 100,000 miles? The word *beautiful* is subjective. Is it luminous or dull? bright or dim? transparent or opaque? silvery, gray, white, or multicolored? Adjectives must be objective and concrete. Dimensions should be quantitative.

Determine what is wrong with each of the following descriptive statements and state what would make it more scientific.

1. Life on earth began a long time ago.

    Too vague. Specifying when life began would make it more scientific.

2. The Grand Canyon is 5,500 feet.
3. The outer layers of the sun are cooler.
4. Steel is less corrosive.
5. The surface temperature of the sun is 11,000°.
6. London is 3,000 miles away.
7. Mount Everest is the highest mountain.
8. A solar eclipse will begin tomorrow at 6 o'clock.

Describing with Adjectives.   Descriptions often involve the use of modifiers. A modifier is a word, phrase, or clause that describes or modifies another word. Modifiers should always be placed as near as possible to the word or words they describe or modify.

Adjectives are used to modify nouns. English adjectives either precede the noun (a *silvery* metal) or come after a linking verb such as *is, looks, seems*, or *becomes* (the metal *is silvery* or the metal *looks silvery*).

The following adjectives are used in scientific descriptions. To show that you understand their meanings, name something each one describes.

1. soluble

    salt

2. flammable
3. edible
4. toxic
5. sour
6. malleable
7. opaque

8. smooth
9. rough
10. fragile
11. transparent
12. rigid
13. flexible
14. viscous

15. elastic
16. odorless
17. volatile
18. dense
19. curved
20. combustible
21. caustic

Adjectives with -ed *and* -ing

Many adjectives in scientific writing are formed by adding *-ed* or *-ing* to verbs. These adjectives are sometimes confusing to students of English as a second language.

Adjectives that are formed with -*ing* frequently indicate a certain action that is performed by the noun or occurs to the noun:

**grinding machine: machine that crushes substances into
small bits
recording mechanism: device that records sound
refining process: process that purifies metals
revolving platform: a stand or surface that turns**

Adjectives that are formed with -*ed* frequently indicate a completed action:

**dehydrated plant: plant that has dried up
magnetized rock: rock that has been made into a magnet
diffused light: light that is spread out
cauterized wound: wound that has been deadened by burning or
searing**

Many verbs can form either -*ing* or -*ed* adjectives. Look at this example of the adjectives *diluting* and *diluted*, which are formed from the verb *to dilute*:

**to dilute: to weaken or thin with water or another liquid
diluting agent: agent or substance that dilutes or thins a liquid
diluted solution: solution or liquid that has been diluted or
weakened**

Using Adjectives with -ed *and* -ing.   Circle the letter of the answer that best completes each of these sentences.

1. A substance that combines metals with oxygen is an _____ .
   a. oxidizing agent   b. oxidized agent

2. Water that has been purified is _____ .
   a. distilled water   b. distilling water

3. A nucleus that is in the process of breaking apart is a _____ .
   a. disintegrated nucleus   b. disintegrating nucleus

4. A device that has been adjusted for errors is a _____ .
   a. calibrating instrument   b. calibrated instrument

5. A device that adjusts other instruments is a _____ .
   a. calibrating instrument   b. calibrated instrument

6. A gas that has been reduced in volume by pressure is a _____ .
   a. compressed gas   b. compressing gas

7. A bar that attaches one moving part of a machine to another is a
_____ .
   a. connecting rod   b. connected rod

8. A base that makes an acid neutral is a _____ .
   a. neutralizing agent   b. neutralized agent

9. A wire that is covered with a nonconductor is an _____ .
   a. insulated wire   b. insulating wire

10. Calcium that has been converted into ions is _____ .
   a. ionizing calcium   b. ionized calcium

Forming Compound Nouns.   Compound nouns are used very frequently in technical or scientific writing. A compound noun is a combination of two or more nouns, such as *space shuttle* or *air conditioner*. In a compound noun the last noun is usually more important. The other words act as adjectives. For example, a *car key* is a type of key, a *pressure gauge* is a gauge used to measure pressure.

Note that in compound nouns, all nouns are used in their singular form. For example, *cancer of the lungs* becomes *lung cancer*. Change each of these phrases into a compound noun.

1. reaction of chemicals   6. preservative of food

2. displacement of water   7. migration of birds

3. compression of air   8. processor of words

4. pump for fuel   9. rain that contains acid

5. density of a gas   10. an addict of drugs

Notice that when a noun is modified by an adjective and another noun, the adjective always comes first. For example, we say *a used machine tool*. Change each of these groups of words to a compound form.

1. container of oil that is large

2. pollution of the air that is excessive

3. pressure of blood that is high

4. defect that occurs at birth and is serious

5. device for the detection of radiation that is powerful

Writing Smooth Sentences.   When writing descriptions, avoid short, choppy sentences. In each series of sentences, combine bits of related information to achieve a smoother flow.

1. Uranus is the third largest planet. It is orbited by many thin rings. It has at least 15 satellites.

   Uranus, the third largest planet, is orbited by many thin rings and at least 15 satellites.

2. Granite is an igneous rock. It is hard and shiny. It is made of several kinds of metals.
3. Calcium is a silvery metal. It is found in limestone, marble, and chalk. It is found in the shells of marine animals.
4. The brontosaurus was a large dinosaur. It weighed about thirty tons. It lived in shallow water. It ate plants.
5. Quasars are starlike objects. They emit radiation. Quasars emit more radiation than entire galaxies.
6. The cerebrum is the largest part of the brain. It controls the senses. It also controls the muscles.
7. Hemophilia is a disease. It is inherited. The blood does not clot properly.
8. The greenhouse effect is the warming of the earth by gases. The process is gradual. The gases are trapped in the atmosphere.

READING SKILLS

Vocabulary Building

   Although it is not a good idea to interrupt a reading or lecture to look up unfamiliar words, at times you will need to consult a dictionary to check the meaning of an important word.

   As soon as your vocabulary is large enough so that you can understand most definitions, use an English to English dictionary. Choose one that is complete enough to cover the words you will need. (Test it by looking up a few words.) A good dictionary contains a lot of information that will help you to understand the correct meaning and use of the word. It may include

1. Part of speech, such as *n.* (noun), *adj.* (adjective), *v.t.* (transitive verb, or verb that can carry an object), and *v.i.* (intransitive verb);
2. Root or derivation of the word (that is, where did it come from?);
3. Synonyms and antonyms;
4. Sentences or phrases containing the word; and
5. A list of the word's meanings. (It is important to look through the definitions to find the one that is appropriate for you.)

   Since many textbooks and technical manuals contain a glossary of terms, always check your book before going to a dictionary.

Word Roots: aqua-, terra-, pyro-, astro-. Study the following list of prefixes and then match the terms at the left below with their meanings at the right. You will not use all the meanings listed.

aqua-: **water**
aquatic = **living or growing in water**

terra-: **earth**
territory = **area or piece of land**

pyro-: **fire**
pyrogenic = **produced by heat**

astro-: **star**
astronomy = **study of the stars and other celestial objects**

_____*f*_____ 1. aqueous solution

_____ 2. rugged terrain

_____ 3. extraterrestrial

_____ 4. pyrometer

_____ 5. pyrotoxin

_____ 6. astrophysics

_____ 7. astronomical

_____ 8. aqueduct

_____ 9. aquarium

a. poison capable of producing fever

b. enormously large

c. outside the earth

d. structure for conveying water

e. rough land

f. watery liquid

g. device for measuring high temperatures

h. inside the earth

i. study of the constitution of celestial bodies

j. tank for plants and animals that live in water

Vocabulary in Context. Circle the letter of the answer that best matches the meaning of the italicized word as it is used in each of these sentences.

1. Few rivers in industrialized areas are *devoid of* pollution.
   a. full of   (b.) without

2. Until the roof is fixed, it will continue to *leak*.
   a. drip water   b. absorb water

3. Asian elephants may become extinct due to insufficient *vegetation* in areas that were once green.
   a. rainfall   b. plant life

4. *Cosmic* rays are dangerous to human beings.
   a. space   b. earth

5. The sun's rays are *filtered* through the atmosphere so that we don't receive their full strength.
   a. concentrated   b. screened

6. In warm climates, water is sometimes heated by *solar* energy.
   a. sun   b. electric

7. The earth's shadow *eclipsed* the sun's light, so it suddenly grew dark on the moon.
   a. blocked   b. absorbed

8. In a desert, the temperature *alternates* between extreme heat and extreme cold.
   a. varies   b. rises

9. The fog *diffused* the lights from the street so that visibility was poor.
   a. spread   b. concentrated

10. Some *lunar* mountains and craters can be seen from the earth.
    a. moon   b. sun

11. The planet Mercury has no *satellite*.
    a. moon   b. atmosphere

12. The space flight was postponed due to *adverse* weather conditions.
    a. favorable   b. unfavorable

Skimming

A good technique for textbook reading is to read the titles and subtitles and turn each into a question. For example, from the title of the passage below, you would formulate the question, "Is the moon a nice place to visit?" and then read to find the answer. This method will help you to focus on the main points, maintain your concentration, and read more rapidly.

Skim the following passage to find its main idea and the kind of information it contains and then answer these two questions. Try to do it all in three minutes.

1. What is the main point of the passage?
   a. The moon is a nice place to visit, but you wouldn't want to live there.
   b. The moon is not a nice place to visit, and you wouldn't want to live there.
   c. Poets don't know anything about the moon.
   d. Scientists don't know anything about the moon.
2. Which of these topics is covered in the article?
   a. the first landing on the moon
   b. the phases of the moon
   c. the climate on the moon
   d. how the moon affects the earth's tides

Reading

The Moon: A Nice Place to Visit?

The moon has been described by songwriters and poets as a place for a romantic escape. We know of course that the moon is actually a very hostile environment for human beings.

The moon is completely devoid of water because the force of gravity on the moon is much less than on the earth. (The moon is much smaller; its surface is about as large as Africa.) The lack of a strong gravitational pull has caused any water the moon may have had to leak out into space over the 4.6 billion years that it has been in existence. Of course, since there is no water, there is also no vegetation. So if you go, bring your lunch.

There is no air on the moon because its gravity is insufficient to retain an atmosphere. Accordingly, travelers to the moon require not only oxygen and water but also protection against cosmic rays that are unfiltered by an atmosphere. No atmosphere also means no weather—no wind, no rain, no clouds.

Temperatures on the moon are quite extreme, ranging from 110° C to −173° C. This occurs because there is no atmosphere to filter the sun's rays when it is shining and then to blanket in warm air when the sun goes down. These extremes of temperature are particularly striking during a solar eclipse, when the earth passes directly between the sun and the moon, temporarily blotting out the sun's light. At such times the temperature on the moon dips very rapidly and then rises immediately as the sun emerges from the earth's shadow. The change in temperature may be as much as 200° C in one hour! This sudden change can cause rocks to shatter due to the alternate expanding and contracting. Thus if you visit the moon, deciding what to wear could be a problem.

There is no twilight or dawn on the moon. Like the earth, the moon does not

shine by its own light; it reflects the light of the sun. Unlike the earth, however, there is no atmosphere to diffuse the light as day becomes night and night turns into day. Changes from light to dark and dark to light occur suddenly.

The lunar sky is black. (Blue sky on the earth is produced by the scattering of blue light in the spectrum by particles of air.) On the moon stars are visible in the daytime, but you would have to shield your eyes from the unfiltered sunlight to view them.

There is no sound on the moon. Sound travels on waves of air molecules. Since there is no air, there is nothing to transmit sound. Leave your transistor home. Also, the moon is not a magnet the way the earth is. You can leave your compass home too.

The moon is a satellite of the earth, revolving around the earth once every twenty-nine and a half days. The moon itself rotates, but it does so very slowly. Therefore the same side of the moon is always visible to us. To get to the moon, you would have to travel 240,000 miles, a distance that is about the same as circling the earth at the equator ten times.

It is clear that if you were making a trip to the moon, you would need to pack more than a toothbrush and a change of underwear. Its adverse conditions would make it very difficult for a visitor from the earth.

Making Inferences. Indicate whether each of the following statements is stated in the passage (*S*), implied by other information in the passage (*I*), or neither stated nor implied (*N*). (Do *not* indicate whether the statement is true or false.)

___S___ 1. The force of gravity on the moon is less than that on the earth.

_____ 2. The tides on the earth are caused by the moon.

_____ 3. A person would weigh less on the moon than on the earth.

_____ 4. The moon has no water or atmosphere because it does not have enough gravity.

_____ 5. It would be difficult to have an argument with someone on the moon.

_____ 6. The moon orbits the earth about once a month.

_____ 7. We always see the same side of the moon.

_____ 8. The earth is 4.6 billion years old.

_____ 9. The temperature on the moon goes up to 200° C.

_____ 10. Human beings could not live on the moon.

_____ 11. Plants could not grow on the moon.

_____ 12. The moon has more extremes of temperature than the earth has.

LISTENING SKILLS

Vocabulary in Context.   Circle the letter of the answer that best matches the meaning of the italicized word as it is used in each of these sentences.

1. The earth travels in an *elliptical* path around the sun.
    a. oval   b. equal

2. We chose the apartment because of its *proximity* to the university.
    a. similarity   b. nearness

3. The trip was difficult because the area was characterized by *rugged terrain*.
    a. rough surface   b. smooth surface

4. Mauna Loa in Hawaii is one of the largest active *volcanoes* in the world.
    a. valleys   b. mountains

5. Antarctica is one of the few unexplored *regions* left on the earth.
    a. areas   b. forests

6. The small amount of water could not *sustain* the large population.
    a. separate   b. support

7. There are *innumerable* bacteria on the dot of this *i*.
    a. few   b. many

8. We enjoyed a *spectacular* view of the comet from the observation tower.
    a. magnificent   b. partial

9. We observed the airplane take off and *vanish* in the distance.
    a. appear   b. disappear

Note-Taking

Some students prefer taping lectures to taking notes. Tapes can be very useful for language learning because you can replay a section that was missed the first time. However, in a science or other academic lecture, tapes do not replace note-taking.

If you tape a lecture, you may be tempted to let your mind wander or "sleep" during the lecture, thinking, "I don't have to listen now, I can listen later." This habit wastes time and prevents you from asking questions on points that may not be clear. Another disadvantage is that without notes, you cannot make the frequent, short reviews that are so important to learning. In addition, when it is time for a test, you will be confronted with many hours of tapes instead of the comparatively short time it would take to review all the notes. Replaying the tapes to take notes at home is also a waste of time.

If taping lectures is permitted and you find this technique useful, by all means use it. But be sure to take notes as well.

Take notes as you listen to the lecture "The Solar System" and then use your notes to complete the next exercise.

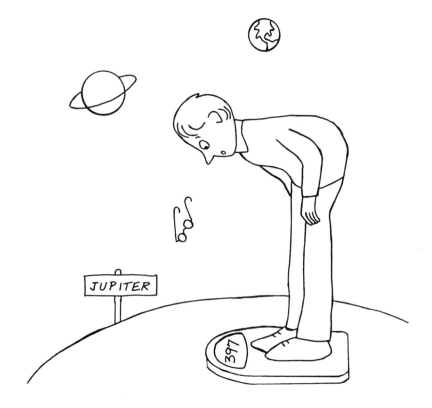

Understanding the Lecture.   Indicate whether each of the following statements is true (*T*) or false (*F*) based on the information in the lecture.

_____*T*_____   1. The sun's gravity keeps the planets in orbit.

_____   2. Venus is the closest planet to the earth and therefore the one scientists can see the best.

_____   3. There is more likely to be life on Venus than on any other planet due to its moderate climate.

_____   4. Mars has changes in climate, like the earth.

_____   5. Recent evidence shows there may be life on Mars.

_____   6. The asteroids are a group of British "rock" musicians.

_____   7. Jupiter may be a ball of gas that is shrinking.

_____   8. The rings of Saturn revolve around the planet like satellites.

_____   9. The farthest planet from the sun is Uranus.

_____   10. No planet has more than two satellites.

_____   11. The tail of a comet points directly toward the sun.

_____ 12. Meteors are stars that burn out.

_____ 13. Meteorites are meteors that land on the earth.

_____ 14. Most of the universe is empty space.

DISCUSSION POINTS

Identify each item from these brief descriptions. Then take turns describing something such as an animal, plant, machine, substance, celestial object, famous structure, or invention to your class, and have your fellow students identify it.

1. a nonmetallic element, used to make computer chips
2. a nocturnal bird that eats mice
3. a poisonous gas, produced by the incomplete burning of gasoline, that pollutes the air
4. an African animal, tall, swift, not a big talker, eats leaves from the tops of trees
5. a drug, stimulant, found in coffee and cola drinks
6. a natural fiber, comes from a four-legged animal
7. a metal that is liquid at room temperature
8. black, soft, crystalline, a form of carbon, and if you don't know yet, look at your pencil
9. a plant, the most abundant form of life, some are harmful, some are harmless, invisible without a microscope, your body is full of them
10. called the red planet, it has polar caps and seasons, located between the earth and Jupiter
11. a household product, made by boiling oil or fat with sodium or potassium hydroxide. Think. You use it every day.
12. elastic substance, comes from the latex of trees, vulcanized (or heated with sulfur) to make it tougher
13. a colorless gas, sweet odor, produces a happy feeling, used as a mild anesthetic, nitrous oxide (Ha! Ha! Did you get this one yet?)

WRITING SKILLS

Describing

A scientific description of a substance or object will usually answer some of the following questions:

1. What are its physical characteristics? (How does it look? Feel? Smell? Taste? What happens to it when heated?)

2. What are its chemical characteristics? (What is it made of? How does it behave or react when it comes in contact with other substances such as water or oxygen?)
3. Where is it found in nature? How abundant is it?

Read the following paragraph which describes the substance mercury and determine which of the above questions it answers.

Mercury is one of a few elements that was known in ancient China, India, and Egypt. Mercury is a lustrous, silvery metal that is a liquid at room temperature. It is 13.6 times as dense as water, freezes at $-39°$ C, and boils at $357°$ C. Mercury does not combine readily with oxygen, but it does react with nitric acid to form mercury nitrate and with sulfuric acid to form mercury sulfate. When mercury combines with certain metals (such as silver, zinc, or tin) the resulting alloy is called an amalgam. Mercury comes from Spain, Italy, and the southwestern United States. It may be obtained by heating mercury sulfide (cinnabar). Mercury is used for thermometers, tooth fillings, and photographic plates.

Writing a Description

Write a description of a natural substance such as rubber, sand, saltwater, wood, air, diamond, straw, aluminum, or carbon dioxide. Your topic sentence might be a definition (a long description is a type of extended definition). In your paragraph, answer as many of the above questions as you can. One way to conclude is to describe how the substance is used.

chapter 12

Predicting
The Weather

INTRODUCTION

The goal of all scientific investigation is to predict the future, and is based on the assumption that what we can predict, we can protect ourselves against. Consider, for example, the number of lives that could be saved by the prediction of natural disasters such as hurricanes, earthquakes, and volcanic eruptions.

Prediction is a part of every field of science. The chemist who develops a new drug must be able to predict its effects—both good and bad—on the human body. The engineer who designs a rocket must be able to predict the effects of adverse weather on the vehicle. The astronomer needs to predict the orbit of a comet, and the biologist must predict the likelihood of a particular child inheriting hemophilia or another genetically linked disease.

Some events can be predicted quite accurately; an eclipse can be calculated to a fraction of a second. Others can only be predicted in terms of probability; the forecast may announce a 25 percent chance of rain tomorrow. However, no prediction of the future behavior of nature is 100 percent certain. The scientist must always be ready to adjust and refine predictions based on new observations.

Short Reading

Read the following passage and find three predictions.

The World Turns

The earth is round; fifteenth- and sixteenth-century explorers like Columbus and Magellan proved it. But there were ancient Greeks who had known this two thousand years earlier. They saw ships descend over the horizon and observed the curved shadow of the earth on the moon during a lunar eclipse. Then, in 200 B.C., the Greek astronomer Eratosthenes noted that at noon on the first day of summer, when the sun was at its highest, its rays shone to the bottom of a vertical well in Syene, Egypt. Yet, on the same day in Alexandria, five hundred miles to the north, it was reported that a vertical post cast a shadow. If the earth had been flat, the post could not have cast a shadow at noon.

The earth spins, or rotates on its axis, once every twenty-four hours, causing us to have day and night. At any given time, the side of the earth facing the sun will have daylight, and the side turned away from the sun will have night. Although the earth is spinning at a speed of over one thousand miles an hour, we do not feel the movement or the wind because everything around us, including the atmosphere, is moving at the same speed. The effect is similar to riding in an airplane. The air moves with you. If you light a match on an airplane, no wind will blow it out.

The earth also revolves around the sun once every year. This yearly revolution, plus the tilting of the earth on its axis, causes the seasons. When the sun's rays are nearly overhead (*not* when the earth is closest to the sun) and the days are long, great amounts of the sun's radiation are absorbed and the weather is hot. For example, from April through September, the North Pole tilts toward the sun and the northern hemisphere experiences summer while the southern hemisphere has winter. Then the North Pole tilts away from the sun and the seasons are reversed. On March 23 and September 21, the North Pole is not leaning toward or away from the sun. If you traveled around the earth on these two dates, you would find the days and nights equal every place you went.

USING ENGLISH TO PREDICT

A PREDICTION

A prediction is a claim that something will happen:

At any given time, the side of the earth facing the sun will have daylight, and the side turned away from the sun will have night.

A PROBABLE PREDICTION

If you light a match on an airplane, no wind will blow it out.
(This prediction will come true if certain conditions are met.)

CONDITION	PREDICTION
you light a match on an airplane	**no wind will blow it out**

A HYPOTHETICAL PREDICTION

If you traveled around the earth on these two dates, you would find the days and nights equal every place you went.
(This condition will also come true if certain conditions are met. But, since the conditions are unlikely to occur—you are unlikely to travel around the world on these days—the prediction is hypothetical. It may or may not come true.)

CONDITION	PREDICTION
you traveled around the world on these two dates	**you would find the days and nights equal**

AN IMPOSSIBLE PREDICTION

If the earth had been flat, the post could not have cast a shadow at noon.
(Here, the prediction would come true if the conditions were met. However, the condition is impossible—obviously the earth is not flat. Therefore, the prediction cannot be fulfilled.)

CONDITION	PREDICTION
the earth had been flat	**the post could not have cast a shadow**

Sentence Patterns

PREDICTION

active: There {will be} an eclipse tomorrow.
passive: The eclipse {will be hidden} by the clouds.

PROBABLE PREDICTION

active: If it rains, we {will get wet.}
passive: If the eclipse is hidden, the photos {will be ruined.}

HYPOTHETICAL PREDICTION

active: If I studied, I $\begin{Bmatrix} \text{would} \\ \text{could} \\ \text{might} \end{Bmatrix}$ pass.

passive: If the eclipse were hidden, the photos $\begin{Bmatrix} \text{would} \\ \text{could} \\ \text{might} \end{Bmatrix}$ be ruined.

IMPOSSIBLE PREDICTION

active: If I had studied, I $\begin{Bmatrix} \text{would} \\ \text{could} \\ \text{might} \end{Bmatrix}$ have passed.

passive: If it had been hidden, the photos $\begin{Bmatrix} \text{would} \\ \text{could} \\ \text{might} \end{Bmatrix}$ have been ruined.

Notes: When writing predictions, remember the following:
1. *The future tense with* will *is used for predictions that are likely to occur. The modals* would, could, *or* might *are used for hypothetical or impossible predictions.*
2. *With if clauses, the subjunctive form* were *is used instead of* was *(for example, If I were rich. . . .).*
3. *Any prediction that is based on a past condition cannot be fulfilled (for example, If the war had ended a year earlier, many lives would have been saved.). Since the war did not end earlier, the prediction cannot come true. Nevertheless, the relationship expressed in the sentence is true.*

Identifying Predictions.   Indicate whether each of these predictions is probable (*P*), hypothetical (*H*), or impossible (*I*).

_____P_____ 1. If sugar is added to water, it will dissolve.

_____ 2. If the volcano had erupted, many people would have been killed.

_____ 3. If the car had fuel, it would go.

_____ 4. If the meteor had penetrated the earth's atmosphere, it would have burned up.

_____ 5. If a fuel, heat, and oxygen are present, combustion will take place.

_____ 6. If the milk were pasteurized, the harmful bacteria would be destroyed.

_____ 7. If neon is given an electric charge, it will glow.

_____ 8. If the apple fell from the tree, potential energy would change to kinetic energy.

Formulating Hypothetical Predictions.   Change each of these probable predictions to a hypothetical prediction, that is, one that may or may not occur. Remember to use *were* instead of *was* in *if* clauses.

1. If we study, we will pass.
   If we studied, we would pass.
2. If a cure is found for leukemia, many lives will be saved.
3. If chlorine is inhaled in large doses, it will be fatal.
4. If mercury is heated to 357° C, it will boil.
5. If the fuel ignites, the engine will start.
6. If it is a clear night, we will see the eclipse.
7. If the wires are insulated, they can be used to carry electric current.
8. If the air temperature drops below 0° C, the rain will turn to snow.

Formulating Impossible Predictions.   Change each of these hypothetical predictions to an impossible prediction, that is, one that is based on a condition that did not occur.

1. If we studied, we would pass.
   If we had studied, we would have passed.
2. If we spoke the same language, we would understand each other better.
3. If we moved the clocks back one hour, we would have an extra hour of daylight in the morning.
4. If the bridge were properly designed, it would not collapse.

5. If the standards were lower, more students would pass.
6. If the satellite were not interrupted, it would continue in its orbit.
7. If the egg cell were fertilized by sperm carrying an *x* chromosome, the baby would be a girl.
8. If he ate a balanced diet, he would be healthier.

Completing Sentences.   Complete the following predictions by filling in the proper form of the verb in parentheses.

1. Plants will not grow if they _____*are*_____ (be) deficient in nitrogen.

2. Many lives would have been saved if scientists _____ (predict) the tornado.

3. A satellite will go into orbit when it _____ (reach) a speed of 18,000 miles per hour.

4. The calcium would melt if you _____ (heat) it to 845° C.

5. When winter comes, the bears _____ (hibernate).

6. If the iron bar were exposed to air, it _____ (rust).

7. If the compound had been an acid, it _____ (turn) the blue litmus red.

8. If the oxygen were cooled sufficiently, it _____ (liquefy).

Creating Predictions.   Complete the following predictions in any logical or imaginative way, using the correct verb form.

1. There would be fewer traffic accidents if __*people didn't drink and drive*__ .

2. People would be healthier if _____ .

3. The air would be cleaner if _____ .

4. School would be easier if _____ .

5. If human beings could fly, _____ .

6. If we could control the weather, _____ .

7. If there were no irregular verbs, _____ .

8. If computers could make breakfast, _____ .

9. If I could go anywhere in the world, _____ .

READING SKILLS

Vocabulary Building: Review

A large vocabulary is an invaluable asset to the comprehension and production of English. To increase your vocabulary:

1. Pay attention to new words, especially those that recur often.
2. Try to guess their meanings from the context of the sentence or paragraph.
3. Use clues such as word parts or related words.
4. Check their meanings with a dictionary or native speaker, when necessary.
5. Select the most important or useful words and write their meanings on cards or notepapers.
6. Carry those cards or notepapers with you and use your spare time to practice the words and memorize them.

Word Roots: -mit, -duct-, geo-, cardio-, psyche-.   Study the list of word roots and then use them to complete the missing words in the following sentences.

-mit: **send, give off**
emit = **give off**

-duct-: **to lead**
deduct = **to take away**

geo-: **earth**
geology = **the study of the earth**

cardio-: **heart**
cardiovascular = **involving the heart and blood vessels**

psyche-: **mind**
psychology = **the science of the mind**

1. Weather information is trans*mitted* _____ by satellite.

2. In ancient times, water was transported over an

   aque _____ .

3. An illness that is brought on by the mind or emotions is described as

   _____ somatic .

4. A muscular action caused by the mind is a _____ motor

   activity.

5. Aluminum is used for pots because it is a good

   con _____ of electricity.

6. A condition in which the heart stops beating is called

   _____ ac arrest.

7. In the spring the high school seniors sub_____ their

   applications to colleges.

8. A metal that can be stretched into wire is described as

   _____ ile .

9. The theory that the earth is the center of the universe is the

   _____ centric theory.

10. A device that measures heart movements is a

    _____ graph .

11. The branch of mathematics that deals with measuring and surveying the

    earth is _____ metry .

Vocabulary in Context. Circle the letter of the answer that best matches the meaning of the italicized word as it is used in each of these sentences.

1. Madame Curie *inspired* many twentieth-century women to conduct scientific research.
   (a.) stimulated   b. required

2. Birds and airplanes seem to *defy* the law of gravity when they fly away from the earth's surface.
   a. obey   b. resist

3. The forecast was for dark clouds that would bring *precipitation.*
   a. heat   b. rain

4. The experiment was *monitored* for errors.
   a. designed   b. observed

5. Weather *forecasts* are more accurate today than ever before.
   a. predictions   b. descriptions

6. There is no *infallible* cure for cancer.
   a. perfect   b. partial

7. The rag was *saturated with* oil.
   a. full of   b. emptied of

8. The seasons of the year recur in *cycles.*
   a. regular periods   b. irregular periods

9. The storm caused *irreversible* damage.
   a. unchangeable   b. changeable

10. The *depletion* of our resources is a twentieth-century problem.
    a. exhaustion   b. increase

11. Mineral *concentrations* in the Dead Sea make aquatic life impossible.
    a. accumulations   b. losses

12. Early storm warnings *averted* disaster.
    a. prevented   b. caused

Scanning

A number of exercises in this book have provided opportunities to practice scanning. Scanning is a reading skill that is useful when looking up information in a reference book. To locate specific information, select possible key words and scan the table of contents in the front of the book, which lists all the chapters in the order in which they appear. Look for the same words in the index at the back of the book. Indexes are made up of key words arranged in alphabetical order.

Take three minutes to scan the following passage and find answers to these questions. (Choose key words for each question.)

1. What are two indicators of the weather?
2. What does a barometer measure?
3. What is the stratosphere?

Reading

Weather or Not

Weather has always intrigued human beings and inspired them to defy nature and try to predict the unpredictable. For centuries farmers watched clouds to determine whether rain was on its way. Mariners studied the changing sky and the drift of the clouds to predict wind directions and storms. Today, the science of meteorology is very complex. It involves gathering information from instruments that measure temperature, air pressure, wind velocity, degree of sunshine, cloudiness, and precipitation. Satellites and electronic computers make it possible to monitor weather information around the world. By studying all the information that is accumulated, the meteorologist determines the general weather pattern over the past few days and makes a prediction about the next few. Weather forecasting, of course, is still not infallible, and may never be.

All weather changes are brought about by temperature changes in different parts of the atmosphere. The sun controls our lives and our weather as it radiates energy to the earth. The areas of the earth near the equator get more heat from the sun than do those near the North and South Poles. The warm air near the equator expands and rises, moving toward the poles. As it cools, it sinks, replacing the cool air on the surface that has moved toward the equator to replace the rising warm air. This unequal heating of the earth causes north and south winds. East-west winds are caused by the rotation of the earth.

Atmospheric pressure, as measured by a barometer, is another indicator of the weather. The amount of water vapor in the air is another predictor. Warm air can dissolve more water than cold air, just as hot tea dissolves more sugar than iced tea. The point at which the air cannot hold any more water is called the saturation point. On a warm day, if the air is saturated with moisture and the temperature drops, the excess water is squeezed out of the air. We see this moisture appearing as dew, fog, or clouds. If sufficient water is squeezed out, we have rain or, at temperatures below the freezing point, snow.

Today there exists a threat to the earth's climate from man-made chemical wastes. Meteorologists have known for a long time that the earth passes through cycles of warming and cooling. The earth has been gradually warming since the last ice age occurred about 18,000 years ago. Recently, however, scientists have become aware of the fact that our technical/industrial civilization may be causing changes in the earth's atmosphere that could alter the weather and that these changes could be very dangerous and irreversible.

One problem is ozone depletion. The stratosphere, or upper atmosphere of the earth, contains a layer of ozone gas that protects the earth from the sun's harmful ultraviolet rays. Recently, ozone concentrations over Antarctica have been dropping at an alarming rate. Researchers have determined that a group of man-made chemicals called chlorofluorocarbons are rising from the earth and destroying the ozone.

A second problem is the so-called greenhouse effect. Carbon dioxide in the atmosphere functions like the glass in a greenhouse, screening out excessive infrared rays and acting as an insulator to prevent heat from escaping at night. Without the protection of the atmosphere, temperatures on the earth could reach the extremes they do on the moon. If we continue to burn fossil fuels, the level of carbon dioxide in the air may increase to the point where it will blanket the earth and cause it to warm to a dangerous level.

It remains to be seen whether this warming trend will continue and, if so, whether scientists will be able to do something about it in time to avert disaster in the next century.

Distinguishing Fact from Opinion.   The American writer Mark Twain once said, "Get your facts first, and then you can distort them as much as you please." Twain was, of course, a humorist and not a scientist, but he knew the importance of identifying facts. Indicate whether each of these sentences represents a fact (*F*) or an opinion (*O*).

____*F*____   1. Weather has always been of interest to men and women.

_____   2. Mariners used to forecast the weather by studying the sky.

. . . Clear and sunny today with no chance of rain. . . .

_____ 3. The science of meteorology is fascinating.

_____ 4. Weather forecasts are a waste of time because they are usually wrong.

__ __ 5. Weather forecasting will never be infallible.

_____ 6. The sun controls our lives.

_____ 7. The earth's rotation causes winds.

_____ 8. Atmospheric pressure is an indicator of the weather.

_____ 9. The earth passes through warming and cooling cycles.

_____ 10. Scientists will never be able to control the weather.

_____ 11. Human beings will never be able to eliminate ozone pollution.

_____ 12. Once the earth's climate changes, it cannot be reversed.

LISTENING SKILLS

Vocabulary in Context.   Circle the letter of the answer that best matches the meaning of the italicized word as it is used in each of these sentences.

1. Geologists can only *estimate* the age of the earth.
   a. guess   b. prove

2. Many people live along the Nile River because the land is *fertile*.
   a. productive   b. unproductive

3. Lands that were *arid* for centuries have been converted into gardens with the use of irrigation.
   a. dry   b. moist

4. Iron is a very *versatile* substance because it can be used in a great number of ways.
   a. abundant   b. many-sided

5. We used a *solvent* to remove the dried paint.
   a. hardener   b. liquefier

6. The *erosion* of the mountainside was due to the heavy winds and rain.
   a. building up   b. wearing away

7. The windshield was *shattered* where the accident victim had bumped his head.
   a. broken into pieces   b. hardened

8. The computer has a word processing *facility*.
   a. capability   b. defect

9. No one has ever invented a *perpetual* motion machine; all machines require energy to keep them going.
   a. permanent   b. slow

Note-Taking Hints: Review

Good note-taking skills are essential to academic success. To sharpen your skills, remember the following:

1. Preread the textbook chapter whenever possible.
2. During the lecture, concentrate on writing down the main points.
3. Use abbreviations, symbols, and shortened forms of words to save time.
4. Don't worry about using full sentences, perfect grammar, or correct outline form but make sure what you write is complete enough to read.
5. Add as many supporting details (such as examples, evidence, and explanations) as possible to help you understand and remember the main points.
6. Write clearly so you can read what you wrote. Don't recopy your notes.
7. Reread your notes as soon as possible after class. Fill in anything you have left out and correct anything that is not clear.
8. Review your notes periodically, especially before a test. The more you review, the more you will remember.

Take notes as you listen to the lecture "The Wonder of Water." Practice the skills you have developed in this course. Then use your notes to complete the next exercise.

Understanding the Lecture. Use your notes to determine whether each of the following statements is true (*T*) or false (*F*) according to the information in the lecture.

___*F*___ 1. The importance of water is usually overestimated.

_____ 2. Water is found in the atmosphere but not underground.

_____ 3. The ocean covers about four-fifths of the earth's surface.

_____ 4. Most of the earth's life exists in the ocean.

_____ 5. Ocean water contains enormous quantities of minerals.

_____ 6. The ocean surface has mountains and valleys just as the land surface does.

_____ 7. The natural color of water is green or blue.

_____ 8. Water is called the universal solvent because it is present in all living things.

_____ 9. Scientists believe that the ocean's salt originally came from living organisms.

_____ 10. Water is typical of other liquids in that it expands when it freezes.

_____ 11. Water heats and cools slower than other liquids.

_____ 12. Water tends to moderate the climate.

_____ 13. The main idea of this lecture is that water is an ordinary liquid.

DISCUSSION POINTS

The Roman orator Cicero once wrote, ''For my part, I think a knowledge of the future would be a disadvantage.'' Discuss how knowing the future could be a disadvantage or advantage. Then use your imagination to make some predictions about the twenty-first century:

1. a scientific discovery that will be made
2. something that will be invented
3. how transportation will be different
4. how communication will be different
5. how people's eating habits will change
6. what men and women will wear
7. how our homes will be different
8. how getting an education will be different

WRITING SKILLS

Predicting

One goal of science is to predict what the world might be like in the future. In the following paragraph, the writer predicts that it will someday be possible to send a letter anywhere on earth in one day or less:

A few years from now, when you wish to send an urgent message, you will purchase a standard letter form on which you will write or type whatever you have to say. At the local office the form will be fed into a machine which scans the marks on the paper and converts them into electrical signals. These will be radioed up the nearest relay satellite, routed in the appropriate direction round the Earth, and picked up at the destination where they are reproduced on a blank form identical with the one you inscribed. The transmission itself would take a fraction of a second; the door-to-door delivery would extend this time to several hours, but eventually letters should never take more than a day between any two points on the Earth. There are, of course, problems of privacy, which might be solved by robot handling at all stages of the operation. However, even the old-style human postmen have been known to read the mail.

Arthur C. Clarke, *Profiles of the Future:*
An Inquiry into the Limits of the Possible
(New York: Harper & Row, 1962), p. 195

Notice how the prediction is made interesting and convincing by both the detailed description of how the system will work and the discussion of a potential problem that might arise. Note also the use of the future tense with *will*. The modal *would* indicates the hypothetical nature of the prediction, and *might* is used to express possibility.

The example paragraph begins with the introductory phrase, *A few years from now*. Other transition words for predicting include *eventually, in the future, gradually, later, after a while, before long,* and *one day*.

Writing a Prediction

Write a paragraph on one of the Discussion Points. Imaginative or creative writing does not demand supporting material to "prove" a point. However, any concrete evidence you can provide will make your paragraph more effective or more believable. For example, if you predict that men and women will dress alike by the twenty-first century, you can support your claim by pointing out that women already wear pants, suits, and ties. Then make sure you develop the paragraph by giving details or examples. Your conclusion could summarize the main idea or express a warning or hope for the future.